# INTERNATIONAL
# MANAGEMENT

## The Authors

**Canning** is a UK-based company whose expertise lies in communication. We help business and professional people from all over the world to communicate effectively with each other across linguistic and cultural barriers. Canning's 80 trainers and consultants run courses at our centres in the UK, Italy and Japan and in another 30 countries on four continents. Over 50,000 people have attended these courses since 1965.

Canning was one of the first training companies to offer specialist cross-cultural skills programmes, tailored for business. All the Canning training consultants who have contributed to this book are members of our cross-cultural skills team. Together they have first-hand experience of working in almost every country in Europe, as well as further afield in over 20 countries, including the USA, Peru, Botswana, Kuwait, Dubai, Iran, India, Korea and Japan. Current cross-cultural skills clients include Cap Gemini, Degussa, Ericsson, Hitachi, Matsushita, Nokia, Nomura, Novartis, Schneider and Toshiba.

# INTERNATIONAL MANAGEMENT

## AN ESSENTIAL GUIDE TO CROSS-CULTURAL BUSINESS

### SECOND EDITION

Gerard Bannon    Vincent Guy
Dr Jehad Al-Omari    Richard Pooley
Bill Reed    Nigel White

of

*Canning*

Edited by John Mattock

INSTITUTE OF DIRECTORS

KOGAN
PAGE

LONDON, UK • NEW HAMPSHIRE, USA • NEW DELHI, INDIA

**Disclaimer**

The masculine pronoun has been used throughout this book. This stems from a desire to avoid ugly and cumbersome language and no bias, prejudice or discrimination is intended.

First published in 1991
Revised edition 1993
Reprinted 1994, 1996
Second edition 1999

Apart from any fair dealing for the purposes of research or private study, or criticism or review, as permitted under the Copyright, Designs and Patents Act, 1988, this publication may only be reproduced, stored or transmitted, in any form or by any means, with the prior permission in writing of the publishers, or in the case of reprographic reproduction in accordance with the terms of licences issued by the Copyright Licensing Agency. Enquiries concerning reproduction outside those terms should be sent to the publishers at the undermentioned address.

The Institute of Directors accepts no responsibility for the opinions expressed by the author of this publication. Readers should consult their advisors before acting on any of the issues raised.

Kogan Page Limited
120 Pentonville Road
London N1 9JN

---

**British Library Cataloguing in Publication Data**

A CIP record for this book is available from the British Library.

ISBN 0 7494 2827 9

---

Typeset by Northern Phototypesetting Co. Ltd, Bolton
Printed and bound in Great Britain by Biddles Ltd, Guildford and King's Lynn

# Contents

# Acknowledgements

There are many books on management and culture. Some are academically detailed, some are statistically rigorous. The emphasis in this book is on practicality and breadth of reference.

We thank the friends, colleagues and clients on four continents who have encouraged us and fed us with ideas, the first edition of this book was in 1991, and their number has grown since then.

We are grateful to the following for permission to quote extracts: Basil Blackwell (*Strategies and Styles*, by Michael Goold and Andrew Campbell); Harper Collins (*Churchill's Black Dog*, by Anthony Storr); William Heinemann Ltd (*Behind the Wall*, by Colin Thubron); the *Independent* (Ties of Anglo-German Friendship, Editorial, 31 March 1990); Martin Secker & Warburg Ltd (*France in the 1980s*, by John Ardagh); John Wiley & Sons Ltd (*Beyond Negotiation*, by John A Carlisle and Robert C Parker, 1989). Every effort was made to trace the copyright holders of 'The Man Who Never Was', by Ewen Montague, which we read in a 1968 Corgi reprint.

Tina Moskal did the illustrations, and also helped greatly with suggestions for editing. Thanks also to Patrick Frean, who drew the pyramid.

In the course of the book, there are numerous generalizations. We have tried very hard to make sure they are not expressions of prejudice, and apologize in advance to any individual who feels affronted. The opinions expressed and any mistakes of fact are entirely ours.

*John Mattock*
August 1998

# Introduction

This book is for you if you are involved in any kind of international business. You might be a marketing executive with a telecommunications group, an export salesperson in machine tools, a progress chaser in civil engineering or a human resources manager in an insurance company – in fact, anybody who works with people from other countries.

In our seminars at Canning we advise business people on how to communicate. They come from many countries and from diverse fields of activity. They work for large corporations, middle-sized niche companies and small consultancy firms. This book draws both on our experience and theirs.

We hope the book will stimulate you to think and act in new ways when you are doing international business. Our particular interest is in how you deal with people face to face – how you communicate.

To give shape to our ideas, we started from the most basic model of antagonism

and decided it was exactly what we did *not* want. So we thought about where it might lead:

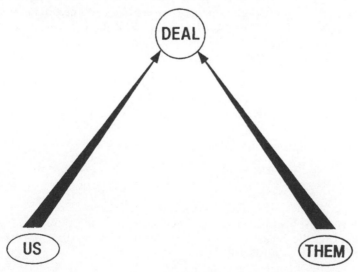

and then broke the process down into a series of steps up the pyramid:

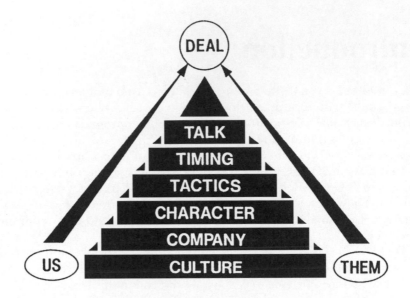

which gave us the chapter headings.

The first three are the Constants: whatever deal you are hoping to strike, it will be influenced by the background Culture, Company style and individual Character of your partner.*

You will need to think deeply about the Constants before moving on to the Transient matters further up the pyramid. The more homework you have done on the Constants, the more effectively you can make decisions about your Tactics, the Timing of activities and the way the Talking (and listening) should be done.

This book can be read and worked with during a flight or train journey. You will need a pencil to do the quizzes and exercises.

---

*Throughout the book, the word 'partner' is used in the continental European sense to mean 'the person you do business with', 'customer', or 'opposite number'. See Glossary on p 135.

# 1

# Culture

Your business partner's background culture – the way of life he was brought up in – will affect his approach to every decision.

There are no foreign lands; only the traveller is foreign.
R.L.Stevenson

## THE WORLD

Communication is a growth business; the world has been shrinking for quite a time. In 1603 it took three days to get a vital message from London to Edinburgh; by 1843 the invention of the telegraph cut this to three hours. Within 40 years the telephone reduced this to threee minutes. Now it can be done in less than three seconds by e-mail. Satellites merge the world's media. Teleconferencing systems link executives across long distances without even the buffer-time of a plane journey. Screen trading enables the banker to deal at the touch of a button, shifting currencies and shares at the speed of light.

Does all this mean the end of the personal touch? Will the business person in the 21st century sit isolated in a bunker, finger on the button? In some areas the answer must be yes: wherever business revolves on commodity-style, single-issue transactions (I buy/You sell/What price?) automation will increase, requiring only a 22-year-old with hot reflexes to pilot the hardware, no matter how many millions are at risk.

But there are other transactions growing in importance and within international reach. Apart from the traditional exporting of tangible goods, deals like the following are mushrooming.

*Start-ups, joint ventures and mergers for access to markets*
● Boots the Chemist opens 40 pharmacy stores in Thailand.

*Takeovers and mergers to gain mass*
● BP merges with Amoco to become one of the top three oil companies in the world.

*Takeovers and mergers to acquire know-how*
● Norway's Nycomed merges with Britain's Amersham to become the world's leading provider of *in-vivo* diagnostic imaging.

*Strategic partnerships to acquire know-how or market access*
● Japanese-owned British-based ICL allies with Microsoft to develop new IT systems.

*Technology transfer*
● Thames Water brings state-of-the-art water treatment to Shanghai.

Back in the 1980s, Kenichi Ohmae, head of McKinsey in Tokyo, advocated a success strategy for international companies and gave it the label, Triad. This meant having a major presence in the three world centres of the US, Europe and Japan. The only way to succeed was to establish insider status in all three, collaborating with former competitors, recruiting and promoting local national staff, and learning about working conditions and markets.

Since then, the focus has widened to include the former Soviet bloc, and more lately China. The Pacific Rim has been badly shaken by economic crisis, with Japan itself in deep trauma. India and Malaysia have become target markets; Indonesia showed promise and has now collapsed. South America beckons. The crystal ball is hard to read, but industries as diverse as electricity, tobacco, chemicals and insurance have recognized that, while the developed world represents today's money, the developing countries contain the seeds of growth for tomorrow.

When the first edition of this book appeared, terms like 'the translational company' and slogans like 'Think Global – Act Local' (Sandoz) and 'Local Insight. Global Outlook' (Hong Kong Bank) were novel appearances in the editorial and advertising pages of *The Economist*; now they are commonplace. The word *glocal* enjoyed a mercifully brief vogue.

But this does not mean the issues have gone away. The muscle of global resources still has to be combined with a sensitive response to local problems and opportunities.

Setting up and following through these more complex arrangements involves getting together with people to thrash out unprecedented solutions to unforeseen problems. A tight grip on the deal itself, or the ability to crunch the numbers correctly, are not enough. The business stands or falls on an understanding of the other side, what motivates them, what their priorities are and how they will change as the relationship matures. In other words, what will make them want to come back for more? What happens when you get out of the bunker, back on the aeroplane, face-to-face on the other's territory? The faces opposite will be from other backgrounds, other cultures than your own. Technology makes it quick and easy to make some kind of contact, but the prizes will go to those who can make good contact.

And more than just playing Mr Nice Guy, making good contact means being more aware.

When a company pushes through a predatorial acquisition, it can expect to lose a number of key staff in the 'victim' company. That is in the nature of things. If too many depart, leaving a worthless shell, there has been a miscalculation, or a failure of planning, on the human side. That planning is even more crucial when the target company is in another country. There are many examples of failure, but here is an all-too-rare example of success.

In 1987, Ericsson won the CGCT takeover in France against competition from Siemens and AT&T, who had been seen as joint favourites. The French ministry negotiator, announcing the winner, applauded the Swedish team as the best communicators and the only ones to have taken the cultural factor into account.

Ericsson is now emphasizing the human element in all its corporate messages: 'It's about communication between people. The test is technology . . .'

## THE INDIVIDUAL

Many people, when they leave home to do a day's work, put on a mask. The thickness of the mask varies from occupation to occupation: we all know, or can easily imagine, a piano tuner or a potter who is at one with his craft – maskless – and we envy such fortunates from time to time. There are certain psychometric tests, usually applied to managers, which are designed to determine how thick the subject's work mask is. The results of these tests provide valuable clues to levels of stress now and in the future. For example, the manager who travels abroad a lot, for short or long periods, is subject to stresses deeper than jet lag, overcrowded itineraries and hangovers, and is likely to have a jaded view of those stay-at-homes who say they envy such an exotic lifestyle.

Airlines understand this well. 'Only by flying Club Europe to over 60 European destinations can you be sure to find the same high standards of service and care throughout the Continent'. A uniform homogenized service is offered to the travelling manager to help him survive the difficult transitions between home (real), work (less real), work abroad (unreal) and social life abroad (frequently quite bizarre).

Managers of many nations have given the label 'Hilton Culture' to the way of life offered. Its adherents have left their roots behind, replacing native values with a bland, predictable Lowest Common Denominator in entertainment, food, conversation, dress, and even ethics. They are all putting on a mask.

- **Hans Weyrich** is a sales manager, based in Hamburg. He is a happy family man, and a regular churchgoer. When his customers fly in to talk business, they expect evening entertainment too. Top of the list is Hamburg's red light district. Hans puts on the mask.
- **Abdelaziz Sabri** is also religious, and Islam prescribes fatalism. He puts on the mask when he leaves Cairo to attend production conferences within the multinational corporation that employs him: what could be less fatalistic than to talk of business targets?
- **Vera Barany** was a qualified auditor under the old Hungarian system, accustomed to the demands of central authority in a centrally planned economy. Budapest is now a thriving free-market scene, and Vera has adjusted her mask.

Insecurity flourishes when human understanding is at risk. And understanding is particularly at risk across a culture gap. To give an illusion of strength, we put on a protective mask that blocks us off from real contact. Meanwhile, the other side is similarly afraid.

'Flight' and 'fight' follow the same channels in the human nervous system. Defensiveness switches over all too easily into aggression. Then communication can break down altogether.

## AS OTHERS SEE US

When we first went out into the world as adolescents, the burning question was 'What do other people think of me?' The classic example is the 15-year-old boy or girl at a party, entirely convinced that all eyes are fixed on their outfit, or the enormous pimple on their nose.

As adults, we can be easily reduced to the same condition, if we are unsure of the ground rules operating in the alien culture in which we are trying to work.

### CULTURE SHOCK – HOW IT FEELS

Take a pen. Write your name five times. Now change hands and do it again. Unless you are ambidextrous, it feels rather uncomfortable. Awkward. Frustrating.

When you are on a long posting abroad, in a culture with which you are unfamiliar, everything you do feels a bit like that: buying a loaf of bread; catching a bus; crossing the street. All the everyday, familiar things still happen every day, but they are no longer familiar.

## EXERCISE

This exercise is taken from one of our warm-ups on cross-cultural training seminars. Appendix 1A, at the end of this chapter, gives the results from one such event where the participants sprang from four different cultural soils.

Imagine you are going to meet someone from another country – preferably a country with which you have had some dealings. When that person talks to compatriots about *your* culture, what generalizations might he voice? 'I've always said about the . . . s, you know, that they are very . . .' or 'One thing you must remember about the . . . s is that they almost always . . .'

Jot down half-a-dozen impressions that you think the citizen of that country has about you and the people of your country.

1.

2.

3.

4.

5.

6.

There will probably be no absolutes on your list. The generalizations that your imaginary foreigner expresses about you and your compatriots will be relative generalizations. If he says that you are a mean or a generous people, he means that you are more mean or generous than his own crowd. This leads us to the question . . .

**What is normal?**

One of the pleasures of international management training lies in the variety of attitudes we meet among the participants. Exercises and case studies that create excitement in Milan sometimes face rejection or produce only bewilderment in Atlanta or Shanghai.

> I was running a three-month management training programme for entrepreneurs in Nizhnii Novgorod – one evening a week. I closed one of the sessions by saying, 'Next week we will be working on Time Management. In preparation for that, please will you keep this piece of paper on your desk? I'd like you to spend five minutes a day filling it in as a record of how you are spending your time.' There they were the next Tuesday evening, all 35 of them, smiling and ready. How many had completed the form? Not a single one!
>
> English consultant in Russia

> We have an international standard system for project management; because so many of our telecom networks involve several subsidiaries in different countries, we need this standard to tie things together. It's my job to travel around giving seminars on how the system works, and make sure that everybody puts it into practice correctly. The key to the system is a series of 'toll gates' – TG1, TG2 and so on. Among the Scandinavians, these tollgates are taken very seriously: if you have to pass TG4 on 10 April, everybody on the team is buzzing about it from the middle of March. In Brazil, they have no meaning – it's just a measurement that people at headquarters take from time to time to make sure we're all working hard.
>
> Swedish corporate trainer

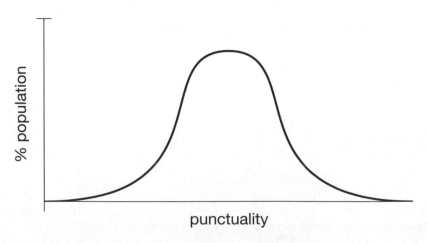

Here the middle section is normal for you in your home culture, while the areas to right and left indicate 'more than you' or 'less than you' of the value on the bottom axis. The English consultant would *not* have expected *all* his trainees to be diligent with their Time Management homework – even at home in Birmingham. The Swede was exaggerating: obviously the Brazilian project teams must be respecting the timetable to some degree, or else they would be breaking too many promises to important customers.

(We have more to say about how attitudes to time vary from culture to culture, in Chapter 5.)

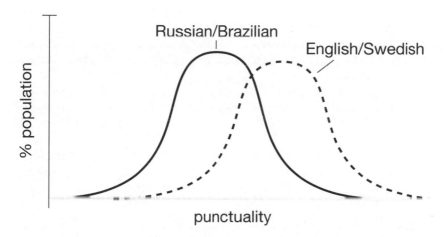

You can change the variable on the bottom axis to *emotionality*, say, or *helpfulness, loyalty* or *thoroughness* . . . It works best with positive attributes.

This is only a way of clarifying your own standpoint, not of learning anything new about the other culture.

Most people are conditioned by liberal society to be ashamed of our generalized views about others. The person who trumpets his views about the 'differentness' of another race is considered to be an embarrassment, or dangerously ignorant but if you are to challenge your own prejudices successfully, you must identify them as clearly as you can, and then test them against the views of others.

## FROM NORMALITY TO STEREOTYPE

Many, perhaps most, Britons would rather be stranded on a desert island with a German than with a Frenchman. Despite enmity in two world wars, the British and Germans believe they have certain values in common, like dependability, straightforwardness, pragmatism and a businesslike approach to life. The French and British tend to see in each other similar vices, like arrogance, selfishness and duplicity; and most Britons cannot understand the French addiction to abstract argument. All such generalisations are tendentious and gratuitous. Yet stereotypes are built on a kernel of truth . . .

The *Independent*, 31 March 1990

How can the *Independent* make these sweeping statements about the preferences of millions of people without including any evidence or supporting argument, and yet guess that the majority of its readers are nodding in recognition?

When it comes to a common understanding of unwritten, unspoken rules about how to get a job done or how to relax over a meal together, Germans do perhaps appear less exotic and closer to the British.

A train across the Channel to Lille takes the British traveller into an atmosphere quite different from home – the fine regard for food, the sexier advertising, the nonchalant driving style. Even though this is still prime beer-drinking country, we feel we are already plugged into the Mediterranean.

Whether or not you agree about the proximity of the Germans to the British or the troubled nature of Anglo-French relations, the *Independent* is talking about something everybody knows and recognizes: our mental picture of national stereotypes.

In fact, stereotypes themselves have had a pretty bad press lately, as have their close cousins, prejudice and generalization. Anthropologists, liberal thinkers and consultants on cross-cultural affairs have been warning us: 'Beware the dreaded stereotype . . . generalizations are vague and deceptive . . . prejudice condemns the foreigner without a fair hearing.'

## PEOPLE LIKE TO BUILD BARRICADES

On a cross-cultural awareness programme run for management trainees with Shell, at the Centre for International Briefing, Farnham Castle, the participants are placed in two teams at opposite ends of an imaginary desert island. From a few scraps of information they are encouraged to build up their own 'culture' – how to solve basic questions of health, wealth, power, family, etc. Then they are invited to join the other team to plan an escape from the island. This throws up a barrage of distrust, bordering on superstition, that the other lot are dirty, diseased, dishonest, degenerate – and all this about the nice people they had breakfast with three hours ago!

Often, such exercises and experiments carry their own lesson for the participants – the presiding referee only has to say 'Well, wasn't that interesting?', and the warning is clear: stereotypes tend to be negative stereotypes. Something in human nature prompts clannishness, and that means bad feelings towards anybody who is not 'one of us'.

'Good fences make good neighbours' said the poet Robert Frost. But the powerful winds of technology and economics are flattening those fences. We have to learn to work well with people who may be very different from our own tribe.

*Eurobusiness* magazine once ran a survey of training services for managers involved in working across national frontiers. The title of the article was 'Learning to be Free of Culture'. So, is the answer to jettison all stereotypes, and walk unbiased through the world, treating each person we meet as unique? Well, this might work in Utopia, but:

> the human tendency towards pattern-making is inborn and inescapable. We cannot see three dots but we make them into a triangle. Human beings have to order their experience as part of their biological adaptation to reality, and the forces which impel them to do so are just as instinctive as sex.
>
> Anthony Storr, psychiatrist

Are stereotypes more than just the result of an instinct? Are they a valid means of encapsulating experience, of joining up the dots?

The *Chambers Twentieth Century Dictionary* definition of the word stereotype is 'a solid metal plate for printing cast from a mould of movable types, a fixed conventionalized representation'. And the real problem with stereotypes is precisely that: they are fixed and conventionalized. They suggest a failure to learn from experience. Generalization entails leaving out the detail. And prejudice is making up your mind before you even get the experience.

## A MORE POSITIVE APPROACH

Scientists build models. Until the 20th century, it was optimistically assumed that science progressed, step by step, nearer to the truth about nature. A scientist was supposed to collect a mass of data and then produce an eternally valid law that explained the data. The more modern view is that science sets up explanatory models which are held to be valid only until proven otherwise – until new data come along to upset the apple cart. In a universe of relativity and quantum mechanics, there is no absolute truth, only models which change or are abandoned as new information comes to light.

When you go to ask the old hand on Kyrgyzstan for advice on working there, he is likely to present you with his model, the key to his system. As you learn to know a culture for yourself, you revise and enrich your own model of how the people in it feel, think and behave, and why they go on that way. Then you are ready to decide how best to channel your own feelings, modify your own thinking and adapt your own behaviour to fit.

## GOODBYE STEREOTYPES

Stereotypes are not always based on mistakes of fact, but they do tend to mistake the part for the whole. They are often out of date, twisted by the media and popular mythology.

Above all, they make very poor small talk with the people concerned.

> France: a land with a thousand sauces and only one religion.
>    England: a land with a thousand versions of religion and only one sauce.
>
> Italian traveller, 18th century

Ever since, the British eater, perhaps too tolerant of poor cuisine, has also had to tolerate foreigners' comments about fish and chips and stale pork pies. These jibes have often been harder to swallow than the food itself. This we might call the 'Mother-in-Law Syndrome'; *I* can criticize the old lady to my heart's content, but don't *you* dare say a word against her.

## HELLO MODELS

Like a set of statistics, your model of a culture enables you to predict behaviour in broad terms, but it cannot guarantee what will happen on any particular occasion. It can help you prepare for what is most likely but may prove unreliable in any one given case. In fact, the next Texan you meet might be small, quick on his feet and modest and the next meal you eat in London might be excellent. If you roll a standard die 600 times, you'll probably score about 100 sixes. But on the 601st throw?

Your model will give you a clear reference point, making deviation easier to understand and setting freak occurrences in context. You adjust the base model once you have accumulated enough exception. The model is the natural starting point. So, how do you develop and apply it?

---

### TELL ME ANOTHER

Claudia Rizzo was heading for New York to promote her bank's services. She knew her product well, and had been hand-picked for her selling ability in a South Italian context. We were running her through her pitch for a particular financial service, and suggested that a certain argument could be reinforced with a concrete example of how another prestigious client had benefited from using the service (naming no names, of course). She balked. 'Where I come from, if I gave a case history at a moment like that, the client would assume that I was inventing it. He wouldn't believe a word.' Not in the US, Claudia; there they expect a concrete example.

---

# LESSONS IN MODEL BUILDING

Cultures are complex. Here we offer some simple approaches, to illustrate how you can use the facts you *already* know to set up a flexible model, in preparation for filtering, focusing and framing new observations.

## *TOPOGRAPHY*

A property dealer revealed the secret of his success in a celebrated aphorism: 'There are only three things that matter about a house: Location, Location and Location. Everything else can be changed.' Much the same could also be said of countries.

Does the unchangeable topography of a country shape the attitudes of its people? Before you read any further, try this simple test.

1. Draw a sketch map of Spain, showing natural and political boundaries. Mark the capital, with its name.

You should have found that fairly easy. If not, you really do owe yourself a couple of hours of browsing in a school atlas!

2. Now do the same for Germany.

Not quite so easy, perhaps? (Look at Appendix 1B, at the end of the chapter, if you want to check your answer.)

Even if you are German yourself, you probably hesitated for a moment at least. Reunification greatly increased the exposure of the map of Germany in the press and on television, but the country's outline remains amorphous and unmemorable.

In fact Germany has hardly any physical boundaries. The Rhine could form one, but the actual border is further to the west. The Alps might serve, but their foothills are well inside Germany, while their heights are Swiss and Austrian. In the north, the sea coast is insignificantly short; Danish and Dutch borders lack even a molehill to distinguish them. The eastern frontier is sometimes news, sometimes history.

Spain, on the other hand, is physically well defined. A nice easy-to-remember square shape, with sea most of the way round, and the Pyrenees to mark the peninsula off from the European mainland. There is a neat chunk bitten out for Portugal, where the political line has for centuries followed the same rivers and watersheds. You might have drawn in that little pointer down towards Africa. Madrid is plumb in the centre.

What does this mean to the average German or Spaniard in the street? What can we infer about their sense of national identity?

Putting it simply, the Spaniard has a clear sense of what it means to be Spanish. In spite of strong regional identities within Spain (Catalans, Andalusians) and in spite of some smouldering disputes (Gibraltar, the Basque country), the main question that runs through Spanish history stems from its position as a peninsula beyond a mountain range: is Spain peripheral to Europe?

One still hears the occasional remark along the lines of *Somos africanos* ('We are Africans'). There is a long history of rejection by conservative forces of any influx that smacked too much of Europe. The 44 *pronunciamentos* (military rebellions) between 1808 and 1936 were largely rejections of this kind. During the Franco years, the gate to Europe was effectively closed, and influences from outside were felt by most Spaniards only in the form of tourism. After Franco, Spain changed more rapidly than any other Western European country. The change lay not just in the establishment of democracy, nor in the modernization of the economy. There was an all-pervading shift of focus towards Europe. Entry into the EC had an emotional force unmatched elsewhere; the Spaniards lept the Pyrenees to become full Europeans. Often heard these days 'I'm European, Catalan and Spanish.'

As for Germany and 'Germanness': lengthy articles appear in the German press there under such headings as 'What does it mean to be German?' Many are intellectually unsure of the answer and that breeds emotional insecurity. There is a saying: '*Ordnung muss sein*' ('There must be order'). That German love of order, system, structure is in part a response to the vagueness of their national borders.

A thoughtful look at the map of a country can suggest quite a lot about the attitudes of its inhabitants. Those simple outlines and contours are a good start to your model building, and give immediate coherence to the scraps of data you have in your head, or pick up during casual observation. Understanding a country for business purposes is largely a matter of unlocking and shaping the knowledge that you already have, rather than embarking on a PhD research project. The map itself will get you asking the right questions and equip you with a strong visual hook on which to hang the answers.

In some cases, similar landscapes yield very different results. For example, the American south-west has much in common with Mexico physically: arid, empty cactus- and petroleum-bearing land. Yet the economics, the personality and the business style of Mexico barely resemble the money, the mores or the manners of Texas and Arizona. Obviously, many other elements – religion, politics, history – go into the mix. Topography does not determine what the people are like; it is a significant contributor to their make-up, and gives you a handy tool to think with. There are other tools available.

---

**DON'T ADJUST YOUR HORIZONS TOO MUCH**

During the 1970s tourist boom, Philippa was doing a summer job at the London Tourist Board. She took a phone-call from Texas. What could she recommend for a two day stopover in England? Well, there was a lot to see . . . Did the caller have any personal preferences?
'Well, I figured on the first morning I might rent a car and drive around the island . . .'

---

A last word on geographical position from the Mexicans themselves, who sum up their situation thus: *'Tan lejos de Dios, tan cerca de los Estados Unidos'* ('So far from God, so close to the US').

## RELIGION

Another model-building instrument, a lens through which to scrutinize the attitudes of a people is religion. The first example is that of Islam in the Arab world. What we have to say is centred on the Arabic-speaking countries – the crucible of Islam – but certain points transcend geography, and hold true for Pakistan, Indonesia, Muslim Africa and elsewhere.

We will take a couple of simple central facts, and see how they can help to build up a model of a people's standpoint and outlook.

**The word Islam means submission**

Literally translated, Islam means submission, but submission to what? To the will of Allah, to the straight path laid down in the Koran (Holy Book), and not to tyranny or temptation. This should take us straight to a primary attitude in Islamic society. Among the six articles of faith in Islam is the belief in **predestination**. This is a deep and complex issue, and we cannot go into it in detail. But it is an issue which can cause tension where Muslims do business with Westerners, who see future business plans as a matter of controlling events, of applying will-power and planning to meet goals. To many Muslims, Westerners can appear to be obsessed with the future to the detriment of the present. To many Muslims, Westerners may appear to be somehow insecure and stressed. Fortune telling, for example, is strictly forbidden in Islam.

There is an Arabic saying: 'Whoever looks into the future is either insane or irreligious'. 'Insha'allah' (God willing) is one of the first phrases that various visitors to the Middle East pick up. It is tagged to the end of many statements about future events, from accepting a dinner invitation to agreeing a deadline on a construction programme.

---

*GETTING CONTEXTUAL*

To most devout Muslims, the use and interpretation of Insha'allah beyond its prescribed meaning (if God wills) is unacceptable. Insha'allah is a sincere and positive promise to perform a task in the future, barring the occurrence of an event outside one's control. It is almost like 'weather permitting' in Britain!

However, in real life, Insha'allah has become the ultimate contextual phrase in the Arabic language, and some would say the most abused Islamic phrase. The range of meanings that Insha'allah can relay is incredible. It could mean a simple 'yes', 'no more' and 'no less'. It could mean 'I hope so'. It could mean 'I will try my best or leave it with me'. It could mean a polite 'no'. The body language, the voice intonation and the circumstances surrounding the particular request or proposition are critical in capturing the real meaning.

---

The life of Muhammed, Prophet of Islam, was full of vigorous activity, so it is clear that 'submission' does not mean passivity. There is a story of a bedouin, who listens closely as Muhammad explains that all things are in the hands of Allah, then asks: 'Is there any need for me to tether my camels at night to stop them wandering?' The Prophet replies: 'Tie them firmly! Then put your faith in Allah.'

A devout Muslim spoke to us about the marketing plans for which he was responsible. 'Do you find any difficulty', we asked, 'in gearing yourself up to push for targets in the future, when your religion dictates otherwise?' 'No problem,' he replied, 'so long as I am working in a team with other Muslims. Together we find the right approach. The difficulty comes when I am working closely with Americans and Europeans. They see the future in such a different way.'

## Koran means recitation

According to some traditions, the Prophet did not write; the words of the Koran, coming direct from Allah through the Prophet's mouth, were written down by attendant scribes. One aim of traditional Islamic education has always been to learn the words of the Koran by heart. Even those who fall short of learning its entirety are equipped with a wealth of quotations and a highly developed oral memory.

In Middle Eastern business dealings today, there is prestige and pleasure to be gained from eloquence; good use of language (preferably Arabic, but also other tongues) is admired. Deals – and differences – are settled by talking. Written communication and contracts – 'pieces of paper written all over' – come a poor second.

---

**AT THE CHURCH**

When I was first invited to a wedding in the UK, I got a few surprises. In the Arab world, a wedding is not between two people but between two families, and everybody gets involved in the arrangements. Being a patriarchal society, the groom pays for everything, including the reception. On a typical wedding in Jordan or the UAE, you will expect to find 200–300 people.

Anyway, once we sat down to watch the ceremony, the priest opened the bible and started reading from it. My reaction was: *Hey, he is a priest. He should know the bible by heart.* I was genuinely surprised to see a man of religion who did not know his stuff! If you go to the Friday prayers in any mosque in the Arab world, the Imam (preacher) may have an index card with a few headings, but you would expect him to know much of the Koran by heart and to be spontaneous. Oratory and eloquence are still admired in the Arab world.

This is particularly relevant to businessmen travelling to the Arab world. They can find themselves in meetings where they are

---

taking lots of notes, while their Arab counterpart is not. The impression each party has on the other is interesting. To the Westerner, the Arab may appear not to be paying attention, especially to detail. To the Arab, the Westerner may appear a bit stupid, he can't keep all this information in his brain. This is not to say that one should not take notes during meetings, but not to overdo it to the extent that it deflects from face-to-face interaction. Finally, to take too many notes in meetings with Arabs may give the impression that there is not enough trust, thus creating the necessity to write everything down.

To use a computer analogy, I would say that if the average Arab has a memory size of 64 MB, your average Westerner would be 8 MB. I know that this may seem unkind to Westerners, but you only have to look at the way most Westerners react to a circular agenda. To most Westerners, the circular agenda is largely confusing and frustrating, and it may indicate lack of focus or a degree of evasiveness or both. To most Orientals, where rote-learning is still common, circularity is an art form, a negotiating tactic and a good way to avoid conflicts.

To push it even further, in cultures where rote-learning and good poetry are still highly appreciated, the spoken word takes precedence over the written word, conversations are allowed to drift; telling anecdotes with hidden meanings adds to the enjoyment, and time is not digital.

Dr Jehad Al-Omari, Canning Consultant

## Ireland – 'The Confessional State'

Those promoting tourism to Ireland emphasize the easy-going charm of the people you will meet there, and the general absence of pressure in the Irish way of life. There is an Irish saying: 'When the good Lord created time, he created plenty of it.' Irish society is fairly forgiving of lackadaisical attitudes. There is an undercurrent of belief, instilled in the country's predominantly Catholic primary schools, that a forgiving God will accept a sincere act of contrition for venial transgressions, and so the transgressor, once having made 'a good confession', can start with a clean sheet.

These attitudes are not necessarily related to the devoutness or otherwise of the individual. Even the most down-to-earth Dublin businessperson, enjoying Ireland's economic renaissance, is given frequent reminders of the Catholic background from which he sprang. Many adoptive Dubliners receive frequent letters from mother, aunt or sister in the country, liberally sprinkled with 'DV' and 'DG' (abbreviations for the Latin forms of 'God willing' and 'thanks be to God').

Such reminders fuel the 'Why worry?' attitude that foreigners often find so beguiling, and which often exasperate those Irish people who are trying to play life's game by more rigorous rules. The native/Catholic Irish identify a zealous adherence to rules and timetables with those alien English who dominated Irish life for centuries.

However, Roman Catholicism among Irish (or Italian, or Polish) migrants to the US has not engendered such carefree attitudes. As a formative influence, religion cannot be entirely separated from our next category, history.

## HISTORY

### How close to Ellis Island?

A great many Americans have an indirect memory of hunger in their family history. Their forebears survived the Atlantic and the ignominy of immigration control on New York's Ellis Island to participate in 'the American way' – material self-improvement through hard work in a huge free market. There was little time for doubt or hesitation with a farm to win from the wilderness, instalments to keep up on the delivery truck, the English language to master and a growing family to provide for.

The following generation – whenever the parents arrived, and from whichever European port – was brought up with those same gritty values. Most now had shoes and full bellies; those who flourished gave priority to their own children's future well-being – through education and through access to the good things in life. (A running theme in American family humour has been the exasperation of the first- or second-generation father at the financial demands of his children.) By the third or fourth generation, a visceral need to succeed in the New World gives way to nostalgia for family roots in the Old.

When dealing with a white American, it is useful to determine what generation he represents. Is Europe the malevolent, prejudiced, no-opportunity hell from which his grandparents escaped, or the quaint, culturally rich home where his great-great grandparents grew up?

For Europeans, the 'American' business person usually means the New York business person, scion of a family that did not join the westward trail, a member of an ethnic group within that cosmopolitan city. The closer that business person feels to Ellis Island, the more likely he is to be a tough, win–lose negotiator, shamelessly in pursuit of the Almighty Dollar.

> It's what America is. It's a nation of immigrants. It's the central event of American history.
>
> Gary Roth, Manager, Ellis Island Project

## TOPOGRAPHY, RELIGION AND HISTORY

We will now briefly consider the cultural make-up of the 'typical' Japanese businessperson, Toshiyuki Suzuki by name, to determine how topographical, demographic, religious and historical threads are woven together in Toshiyuki's attitudes.

Most people know that Japan is overcrowded (only 30 per cent of the land-mass being habitable). Few westerners recognize the historical aspect of this topographical truth: the fertile coastal strip of Japan has been packed solidly with humanity for many hundreds of years. There is no Japanese word for 'privacy', unless we admit the imported *'puraibashi'*. Like his ancestors, Toshiyuki must find ways of keeping himself to himself without the benefit of a solid bedroom door to close behind him.

Those ancestors despised and feared foreigners. For over 250 years (the Tokugawa era), while Western European cultures were evolving liberal democracies, Japan remained cut off in its feudalism – until 1868.* The echoes of xenophobia and a need for clear hierarchy are still strong in Toshiyuki's life.

The third thread is religion – or rather the lack of it. At the beginning of the Tokugawa period, all religious and philosophical works were banned – bar the Analects of Confucius. The permitted code was a mercilessly rigid pecking order, a system of conduct based on duty (*giri*) as opposed to individual human rights, and a relativist ethical outlook – no Ten Commandments recited from the pulpit in 19th-century Japan. Behaviour was, and still is for Toshiyuki, largely determined by the company being kept.

Toshiyuki learnt at his mother's knee to modify his language according to the status of those present; he is under constant social pressure to keep his emotions to himself; his employers encourage ever more dedication to the harmony of the group. Each of these cultural sketches contains outlined above a few basic facts. More important are the connections drawn within each piece between those background facts and the attitudes typical of the culture in question. As this book progresses, we shall consider how such attitudes affect behaviour, particularly in business, and suggest how you might modify your own behaviour accordingly – improving your chances of reaching your business goals.

Building flexible models upward from *facts*, through *attitudes*, to *behaviour* is more useful than accumulating random 'handy hints' regarding business cultures. It helps to know that a Japanese business card should be received in both hands and venerated, or that your Arab business partner might be offended if you pass him something with your left hand. But such snippets of good manners mean a lot more if they can be set in a context.

---

*In 1853, the US Navy forced Japan to open its gates to international trade. This led directly to the collapse of the Tokugawa order.

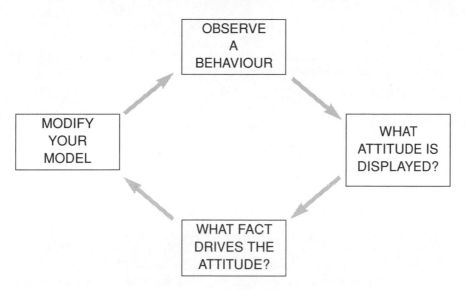

- *Facts*: Population density; economic history; family/tribal structure; religion; topography; climate; laws; news and information media.
- *Attitudes* (and values): Business before pleasure or vice-versa? Naturally rebellious or happy subordinates? Spiritual or materialistic? Ingenuous or secretive? Cosmopolitan or parochial?
- *Behaviour*: Do they stick to the agenda? Make jokes about the boss? Invite you home for dinner? Insist on having everything in writing? Welcome challenges – or hide from them? Keep promises – or let you down?

This process is subjective; the model you build will be *your* model. There are links between background facts, the values of the people, and the way those values make them behave. Although you will never prove those links scientifically, your model will hold everything together. Without it, all your observations will remain a random and unconnected jumble.

The whole exercise must be driven by curiosity. In 1980, a curious traveller was motoring across White Russia (Belarus):

> Already the country . . . was slow, impersonal and absolute. I could not help wondering what effect such isolation might have on its inhabitants . . . Was the easy Russian submission to God or tyranny, I wondered, the result of a people crushed by the sheer size of their land? Could it be the meandering, mystical, rough-hewn qualities of the Russian psyche – Russian novels, Russian music – the unwieldy immensity of Russian bureaucracy . . .
>
> But this froth of irresponsible questions subsided unanswered at a sign which said 'Minsk Campsite' . . .
>
> Colin Thubron, *Among the Russians*

## EXERCISES

1. Try to extrapolate from the following background facts a pattern of attitudes in the people who come from the countries listed:

> Finland – lakes and forests;
> Hungary – land-locked;
> France – Descartes and *la raison*;
> Belgium – two languages;
> England – Industrial Revolution
> India – the caste system;
> Argentina – the Italian diaspora;
> Canada – the northern neighbour of the US.

2. Experiment with another analytical instrument. Take a culture you know quite well, and see what patterns emerge when you look at it through a pair of spectacles borrowed from a meteorologist.

For example, does Swedish introspection have anything to do with long, dark winters? When a North Italian calls the southerners in his own country unreliable, is it connected with the sunshine?

3. Let your curiosity take new paths.

- A colleague of ours, unversed in the ways of Islam, read in draft the paragraphs about the Koran and the oral tradition. She immediately asked: 'Do the women in Islamic cultures share in this passion for eloquence, or is it a male preserve?'

- Our 'Ellis Island' model was challenged by a Puerto Rican, who quite reasonably accused us of oversimplification. A fuller essay on the US would need research on the ethnic groups which did not travel from Europe. How does the *facts attitudes behaviour* sequence apply to them?

- Once you have started to build your model of a culture, you can augment and enrich it by asking questions of it, challenging it, and thinking laterally. And by having fun with it!

### THE STORY OF LUCY

(A light-hearted self-analysis. Its relevance to understanding other cultures is made clear in Appendix 1C at the end of this chapter.)

There is a river. Beside the river, in a little house, lives Lucy. Lucy is in love with Peter (who lives on the other side of the river), and she doesn't know what to do. So she goes to her friend William and asks him.

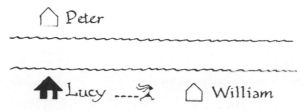

'Perfectly simple', says William. 'If you love him, go and tell him.'
'OK', says Lucy, and she goes to the river, where she meets David, the boatman. 'Please will you take me across the river, David?'

'Of course. But what time do you want to come back again?'
'I don't really know', Lucy confesses. 'Why do you ask?' David explains that he has a contract downriver at six o'clock, and that if Lucy wants a ferry home, she must be at the landing stage before that time.

They cross the river. Lucy goes to Peter's house and knocks on the door. Peter opens the door. Lucy says, 'Peter, I love you.' Peter cannot resist the temptation. He makes love to Lucy.

When she recovers from her delirium, Lucy becomes upset at the thought that Peter has taken advantage of her. She runs out of the door, along beside the river, and to the house where Michael lives.

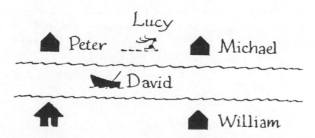

Now, Michael is in love with Lucy, so when he opens the door and sees her there so clearly troubled, he says, 'Come in, you poor girl, and tell me all about it.' Lucy goes in and tells him all about it. Michael becomes upset in his turn, and asks Lucy to leave.

She arrives at the landing-stage at one minute past six. David has cast off, and is rowing away from the jetty. Lucy calls to him, 'David, please will you take me home?' David points to his watch. 'I'm sorry, Lucy. I warned you.' And he rows away downstream.

Lucy decides to swim home. In mid-stream, she drowns.

There are five characters in this story. Your job now is to rank them, one to five, in descending order of responsibility for the death of Lucy. In other words, if you think Michael is the most responsible, enter him in slot I, and work your way down.

1 _____

2 _____

3 _____

4 _____

5 _____

Now turn to Appendix 1C.


## *VALUE GRID*

Now here is a simple way of crystallizing a model of another culture and comparing it to your own.

In the following table Column 1 is for your own culture, Column 2 is for a culture you know fairly well, and Column 3 is for a culture you know only a little.

Put the names of those cultures at the top of the columns.

Next, picture in your mind 10 people from your home culture who are more or less your social equivalents – similar age, similar education, similar occupation. Now look at Question 1, Column 1. If you think four of the compatriots you have chosen go regularly to church (or mosque, or temple, or shrine), enter '40%' in the box.

Now picture a group of 'similar' people from your chosen culture in Column 2, and enter a percentage. And so on. Sometimes you will have knowledge to support your scoring, sometimes you will be relying on intuition or guesswork. You will find a commentary in Appendix 1D

## Culture

|  | Home culture | Known culture | Little-known culture |
|---|---|---|---|
| 1. Active in religious observance | % | % | % |
| 2. Materially ambitious | % | % | % |
| 3. Family-minded as priority | % | % | % |
| 4. Fond of alcohol as social lubricant | % | % | % |
| 5. Earnest about the company | % | % | % |
| 6. Mobile from job to job | % | % | % |
| 7. International in outlook | % | % | % |
| 8. In awe of authority | % | % | % |
| 9. Respectful of qualifications | % | % | % |
| 10. Egalitarian/ feminist | % | % | % |

# APPENDIX 1A – NOTES ON 'AS OTHERS SEE US'

The training session was a weekend event, organized to promote understanding within a new East European business venture.

The participants were split into four mono-cultural groups to discuss the way they thought the other cultures perceived them.

Each group was asked to report back with six characteristics – adjectives or short phrases.

The American list:

● arrogant

● enterprising

● superficial

● money-oriented

● open

● uncultured.

The German list:

● punctual

● meticulous

● neat

● stubborn

● hard-working

● fond of beer and sauerkraut.

The British list:

● phlegmatic

● imperialist (they were the senior partners)

● isolationist

● principled

● tenacious

● drily humorous.

The Hungarian list:

● diligent

● proud

- gifted
- pessimistic
- undisciplined
- born victims.

With these 24 epithets pinned to the wall, the questions to be dealt with were: 'Have we got each other, or ourselves, wrong in this or that respect?'; 'Is this or that attitude actually an asset to the team?'; 'Should we/can we modify this or that aspect of our behaviour in the name of harmony?' Then they started to build their team spirit.

We were recently running a workshop for the European headquarters of a major US-based multinational company. The European HQ is located in the UK. Although the boss is French, most of his subordinates are British. Our brief was to try and help these staff to gain a better understanding of American business culture. So, we asked if American managers – who were on secondment to the UK – could join us. It soon became clear that the problems existing between the US and UK operations had little to do with a lack of understanding of each other's culture. Things were going wrong because neither side realized how they were perceived by the other. We asked the Americans and the British to give their perceptions. It took time for the truth to come out. When it did, it was a revelation to both sides

The American image of the British can be summarized as follows:

- always talking about problems, not solutions
- focusing on what has happened and not on what will happen
- gloomy and depressing, even when they are giving good news
- rude and disrespectful
- badly prepared.

The British image of their American colleagues was just as negative:

- forever over-optimistic
- not prepared to analyse a problem so as to find workable solutions
- boastful and superficial
- not prepared to disagree with a superior even when he is wrong
- badly prepared.

The communication style of each side – the way they manifested themselves and their ideas – seemed the obvious place to start. At the next quarterly report meeting in the US, one of the British managers made a deliberate effort to sound more enthusiastic, and emphasize future possibilities rather than analysing the past. The Americans were impressed, and a budget increase was granted.

Prejudices are dangerous, but there is no smoke without fire: national reputations grow and spread because of the behaviour of the people, and there is such a thing as 'typical' behaviour in a culture. Simple labels – 'French love of logic', 'Italian obsession with style', 'German respect for law and order' – give useful guidance.

If your foreign partner sees a fault in you and your compatriots, then you must face and accept that as a fact. Then the choice is yours – either to ignore the criticism and remain 'true to yourself' or to modify your behaviour and gain greater approval.

# APPENDIX 1B – SKETCH MAPS OF SPAIN AND GERMANY

Homeland
of a citizen
of Madrid

Homeland
of a citizen
of Berlin

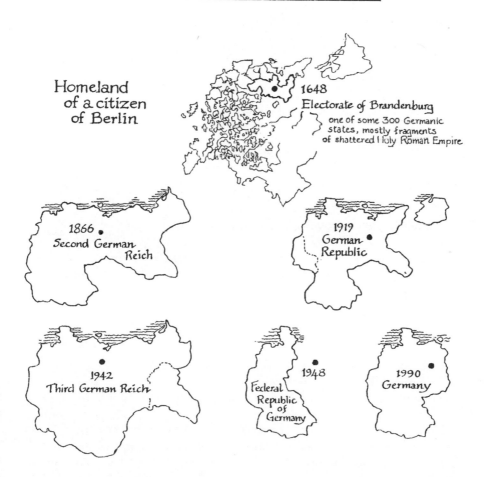

# APPENDIX 1C – COMMENTARY ON 'THE STORY OF LUCY'

This is an old Victorian smoking-room exercise – the sort of thing gentlemen diverted themselves with over brandy and cigars when the ladies had withdrawn after dinner.

The key to the game is primitive, and bears little relation to any modern psychological theory. Thus warned, read on.

Each of the five characters in the story represents a human quality. The order in which you rank them reflects the importance that you attach to each of those qualities. The lower on the scale of responsibility, the more important that characteristic is to you. If you blame character X for Lucy's death, you are saying that you despise or reject his motives.)

Cast in order of appearance:

| | | |
|---|---|---|
| Lucy | represents | *Love*; |
| William | represents | *Wisdom*; |
| David | represents | *Duty*; |
| Peter | represents | *Passion*; |
| Michael | represents | *Morality* (or so the Victorians felt. Why do you |

think he kicked Lucy out? Your interpretation reflects your culture.)

So, according to the rules of the game, if you decided on the ranking:

William
Peter
Lucy
Michael
David

you attach little importance to wisdom and a great deal to duty.

Of course, you project a lot into the story as you read it: How old was Lucy in your mind's eye? Was the river a stream with ducks on it, or an icy torrent? When she called out to David, was she pleading with tears in her eyes? – we never said so.

## *CROSS-CULTURAL INTERPRETATION*

Ponder for a moment how cultural background might affect a person's responses to the sad tale of Lucy.

We have run this exercise many times on training courses, with groups of mixed nationality.

On one notable occasion, the participants in the test were nine Swedes and three Venezuelans, all working for the same company, whose headquarters is in Stockholm. The Scandinavians (men and women) unanimously placed Lucy at the head of the list, while the South Americans all had her at the foot ('But poor little Lucy!').

And the same spread was true in Italy, where none of the Neapolitans in the group could see Loving Lucy as anything more than a helpless victim, to the bemusement of their Milanese colleagues – who agreed with each other that she should have shown more sense, and deserved her fate.

Similarly, David (Duty) is usually placed high on the list by Latins ('For a lousy contract he condemns a beautiful girl to death!'). The classic German response is that he had a job to do, that he gave Lucy fair warning, and that he made the right decision in the circumstances. (*Ordnung muss sein.*) Yet within Germany, there is likely to be disagreement between, say, a young Bavarian and an older Prussian.

Some say, when asked to allocate responsibility for Lucy's death, that there is simply not enough evidence to go on. (Perhaps you reacted that way yourself.) This shortage of data often leads to what we call 'The Lawyer's Answer', placing Lucy herself first (she was alone when she died), followed by David (the last to see her before the drowning), and then Michael, Peter, and William (in reverse order of appearance in the story as told). In our experience, the Cartesian-minded French person is likely to choose this option.

William rarely gets the blame: few people say 'It was his fault – he started it all.' There was a Swiss-German once who guessed that the rest of the group would place Lucy first for what he considered to be liberal/feminist reasons. He succeeded in provoking them by blaming William above all, on the grounds that 'he missed his opportunity'.

And of course, culture changes over time. Western women now not only hear the story of Lucy without blushing, but place her top of the list as responsible for her own actions.

## APPENDIX 1D – COMMENTARY ON 'VALUE GRID'

As you filled in the form, you were making certain assumptions about what the questions meant regarding your 'home culture'. You probably transferred something of those assumptions to the 'foreign' cultures.

If you are from Caracas, travel often in the US, and have never met a Greek, you know with some precision how Venezuelan middle managers view their companies. You have made a reasoned estimate of the same value among your North American partners, and pondered your ignorance about the Greek attitude.

This exercise is useful as a framework for identifying such areas of ignorance. You are reasonably equipped to do business in a foreign culture when you have a clear view on at least half the questions.

# 2

# Company

During your dealings with him, your business partner will be the embodiment of his company, division or department. Consider how his 'company culture' is different from yours, and what you might do to bridge that gap.

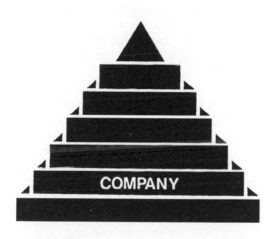

## COMPANY CULTURE

Late in the season a few years ago, during a touring holiday in Crete, we took a taxi ride to a remote beach. We asked the cabbie how business had been during the summer.

'Not good. About 30 per cent down on last year. We rely quite heavily on British tourists, you see. You've had a hot summer in England, so a lot of people there have spent their holiday in the garden. Cheaper for them, too – which is important when your interest rates are so high. What is it now? Fourteen per cent? That's a lot on a mortgage, and the English are very keen to buy their own homes. And on top of all that, the Turks are spending a fortune promoting Turkey as the smart place for a cheap holiday, so Crete is less fashionable these days.'

Many executives are involved in international business without that much understanding of market forces. We cannot step up to the second level of our pyramid without tipping our cap towards the market, which operates in the context of 'Culture', and sets the context for 'Company'.

The entrepreneur, managing his own affairs from top to bottom, cannot afford to ignore such factors. If you are a cog in a bigger machine, you can only gain if you emulate the successful entrepreneur.

> Make all your decisions as if you owned the company.
> Robert Townsend, former president of Avis

## QUESTIONNAIRE

The following questionnaire is a simple microscope to help you look at your company (or your suppliers, or your customers, or your competitors, or your bankers . . .), and perhaps find some pattern in the movements of the bacilli on the slide. What factors underlie the behaviour of employees?

In completing the questionnaire, bear Townsend's advice in mind: place yourself in the position of the CEO, or guiding spirit of the corporation, and answer the questions as he would.

After the quiz, we will report on how executives from various companies have responded to it.

For each section you have a total of 10 points to distribute among the statements (a), (b) and (c). The points can be spread over two or three statements, or you can concentrate on a single one.

The questionnaire is written in the first person ('my company . . .', 'we have subsidiaries . . .'), but remember it can be applied to another company – perhaps the one you are about to have dealings with.

In Column 1, enter 'the way my company really is'; Column 2 is for 'the way my company should be', or 'the way my company seems to be going'; in Column 3 you can put in scores for 'the other company'.

| | | 1 | 2 | 3 |
|---|---|---|---|---|
| **1.** | My company is efficient because:<br>(a) we set up the right systems<br>(b) we trust our people<br>(c) we are flexible and responsive to client needs | | | |
| **2.** | We hire the right people because:<br>(a) managers involved in recruitment have a good nose<br>(b) we define precisely the type of person we want | | | |

(c) candidates are helped to understand the values of the people they would be working with before they decide to join

3.  We handle public relations successfully because:
    (a) we have a clear sense of our identity
    (b) we have an open door to clients and press
    (c) we make efforts to get a message across to the community and the market

    1 | 2 | 3

4.  We solve problems and make decisions:
    (a) by thinking things over in isolation
    (b) by going to the right specialist
    (c) by pooling ideas from many sources

    1 | 2 | 3

5.  Innovation in products and organization:
    (a) is not a primary concern; we are already leaders in our field
    (b) is a challenge; our past and present success can make change more difficult
    (c) is a natural process; our current success stimulates new approaches

    1 | 2 | 3

6.  Top management get results because:
    (a) there is one strong person who makes all the crucial decisions
    (b) there is a group of experienced people at the top who know where the firm is heading
    (c) it is receptive to signals from outside and from below

    1 | 2 | 3

7.  Leadership throughout our organization is effective because:
    (a) managers give clear, detailed instructions and monitor progress closely
    (b) managers work closely with their teams and set the right example
    (c) managers set clear goals but let subordinates decide how to reach them

    1 | 2 | 3

8.  Human relations are good because:
    (a) we do not mix business with pleasure
    (b) we socialize mainly with our peers
    (c) senior and junior people feel free to relax together

    1 | 2 | 3

9.  Our activities are international in that:

    1 | 2 | 3

(a) we export a lot
(b) we have marketing outlets in other countries
(c) we have subsidiaries with full functions in
other countries

| | | |
|---|---|---|
| **10.** We are an international team in that: 1 | 2 | 3 |

(a) we employ local staff abroad for some
functions
(b) operations abroad are led and managed
by local nationals
(c) the corporate board includes members
from many countries

## COMMENTARY AND FINDINGS

The questionnaire above draws heavily on *Beyond Negotiation* by Carlisle
and Parker. We used it as a basis for interviews with about 100 managers
from various industries and countries.

We set out with the following thesis, derived in part from Carlisle and
Parker: a company with the right culture will have an advantage in international competition; the right culture is one that favours creativity, fair-
ness and open communication.

We half expected the underlying theme to be obvious to the respondents: surely most of them would point to option (c) in every case and say
'that is where my company would like to be'. In fact, the results were far
more complex, giving some indication of the diversity which people
bring to the business of running a business.

The results, from which we present a selection below, also support the
theme of this book: *business cultures are deeply embedded in country cultures*.

(*Note:* The companies and our respondents preferred to remain
anonymous.)

---

**Respondent A: British manager in the central office of a petroleum
multinational.**

1.      We've been fortunate – it's a good business to be in, and many of
        our high-risk opportunities have paid off. Demand may fluctu-
        ate, but it's always there, and on a far greater scale than could
        have been dreamt of when the company first began. We have a
        long history and we take a long-term view. With a five-year
        rolling plan and a scenario that extends 20 years ahead, we
        really do have a strong vision of the future. Systems, yes, but that

suggests something too rigid. There's a set of business principles, a way of projecting a vision from the centre, giving people confidence to make the right decision.

2. It takes a long time to build a chief executive. He has to pick up an awful lot in a short time, if he's going to be effective as a top manager by his late 40s. Say he's had 25 years in the company – that's very little indeed in a long-term business like ours. It's unlikely that you'll reach the very top unless you start early. So we have to pick the very best and we pick them young. Recruitment tends to look for 'people like us', though some mavericks do slip through and serve an important leavening function.

3. It's a commodity business, but a highly competitive one. That means image really counts. The way we handle PR affects our business performance very directly: for example, in getting government support at the exploration stage; raising capital in financial markets; even cash sales at the petrol pump. The wrong move or the wrong message on sensitive issues like the environment could make mincemeat of a lot of carefully-made plans.

   I would say we're good with the institutions, with professionals and probably with schools too. A bit patchy with the public at large – which is the most complicated. But we maintain a healthy market share, and that suggests we're reasonably well regarded.

4. There's a kind of looseness in the way we go about making decisions – it can seem tedious at times, but it can also work miracles. On a major issue, the end of the process will be unanimous acceptance. Underlying the consensus is that central vision of where the company is going. For most matters there are specialists within the company, but we have called in outside consultants, for example, on the issue of organizational change.

5. Innovation on the product side is evolutionary, and we spend heavily on research. But the business environment has changed dramatically and we've had to change the organization to meet it. The 'Seven Sisters'* no longer have predominance in the industry. We're now in competition with the producer nations themselves. The era of country-club culture and straight-line economic projections is over. We have to be more flexible, more open.

6. We have good antennae: lots of people constantly listening for signals all around the world. Authority is delegated to the operating countries. It's non-autocratic.

---

* BP, Chevron, Esso, Gulf, Mobil, Shell, Texaco.

7.  Signals get passed, often through informal networks. I'll pass a message to someone overseas to think, to follow a lead from that central vision. It might be just a question 'What have you done about that?' or advice like 'This is unlikely to gain support'. Because managers move around a lot, a powerful network builds up. People get to know each other and that aids communication.

8.  There's a loyalty common to all and a fair deal for everyone. The wife of one of our senior managers in China, who disappeared during the Cultural Revolution, spent many years in jail, and recently turned up in our Hong Kong office. Everything was laid on for her, pension on tap, she was 'one of us'. It's all part of the long-term view.

9.  It was an international company from the very start. Today, we have more interests in more countries than any of our competitors. Shareholders are also very widely spread around the world.

10. Posting managers to different countries is part of their training and a way of consolidating the communication network. There are many nationalities working at central office, as well. In my case, I'm British, with other nationalities directly senior and junior to me. All this leads to speedier decisions and, I believe, better decisions. Movement may mean losing some depth and client contact, but it means we can call on a very rich pool of talent. For a decisive post, we can match not only qualifications and experience, but temperament – we can bring in a market-builder, a consolidator, a soft-spoken diplomat, or whatever, from anywhere in the world. The original nationality of the company has been pretty well lost in this international melting pot.

---

**Respondent B: Frenchwoman providing support to front-line bankers in international work at the Paris branch of a US bank.**

1.  Corporate culture plays a big part in our bank. On joining, at any level, everybody goes through a one-week seminar about the aims, the driving force, the history of the bank. And there's a motto about quality which is pushed pretty hard. We operate in a specific niche with top-rank clients only. We have to fit our service precisely to what the client wants – tailored solutions. So even junior people, who may never see the client, have to understand this special approach.

2.  We do a lot to get this approach across to people before they join. Satisfying the client is very hard work, which not everybody wants. There are plenty of easier jobs. But here you get the

chance to follow your own initiative and to work with highly motivated colleagues. Definition plays a part, too: we need people with good contacts in the market, which includes, for example, graduates of the top business schools.

3.  Within the bank there's a strong sense of belonging, in both a local and a global sense. People like to talk about how old-established we are, what we did in the crash of 1929. It's rather surprising for the French, who tend to have a more individualist attitude to work. The French style is to be dedicated to the profession and the career, rather than the corporation. The bank does no cold selling and only advertises selectively; we work through contacts and connections and build up long-term relations.

4.  Networking and pooling of experience flow freely, even from one country to another. The overall structure for decisions is that each subsidiary has a wide measure of freedom, but must report upwards in great detail. The same goes for each department or team within the subsidiary.

5.  Adapting to the client means constant innovation. That's the heart of the business. Our services are expensive – if we don't come up with new ideas, our clients will go elsewhere.

6.  Top management at the US end are quite visible. We know their names and most of the faces. When someone new joins the board, we get a big memo, describing his career and his aims. Until recently, there was a single strong man at the top. He was particularly good at representing the bank, almost a symbolic leader, though also very receptive. What we see currently is a strong group in control.

7.  At my level, I can solve some problems myself, but I can also go up for advice without any loss of face. I can call a senior person in the US, once, but not too often. If need be, I can ask my superior in Paris to use his authority to help me.

8.  In spite of the sense of belonging, human relations are not always that smooth. The atmosphere is highly competitive. A lot of young people have been brought in recently and there's rivalry among them. On top of that is a generation gap: with the 40- and 50-year-olds who joined in easier times. They're still needed for cultural continuity. But there are tensions which you must expect in a fast-moving climate.

9.  Our market positioning means we are fully present in the world's financial capitals, but not at all outside them. We have no pres-

ence in the Third World. And our experiments with offices in the French provinces didn't lead anywhere. Our customers are either in the big city, or they like to come there.

10.   The subsidiaries are led by locals, but with very close reporting to the US. The board was 100 per cent American until very recently when an Englishman made it. That was quite a breakthrough.

---

**Respondent C: Board member, Spanish manufacturing company.**

1.   We are something like an industrial boutique, specialists in high quality product, limited volumes, near the top of the price range. But we set out in the 1970s with a very different aim: to build the world's largest factory in our sector. The crisis years before Franco's death put a stop to that, and subsequent deregulation kept up the pressure. Massive staff cuts had to be put through in a climate of fear. Just as a serious illness can make you give up your bad old habits, a few of us clearly saw the need for a new way of thinking. What came in was quality, open communications, commitment to training.

2.   For the last 15 years, it's been mainly reverse recruitment, laying people off. All done on a straight seniority formula agreed with the unions. The average age of the workforce is now around 45. Currently, we hardly recruit at all. If we do, we're more interested to know *their* values than to explain ours.

3.   As we're a subsidiary, our parent has the main PR responsibility. It's out of our hands and we're not always happy with the way they handle it. But the market is aware of our quality.

   Within the company, the quality programmes have built a strong sense of identity. There are 56 quality circles in a workforce of 1 500. An effective detail is the suggestion box for slogans, which are then used around the works, in the local press or even on the product. But an open door policy is something I don't believe in.

4.   In a crisis, thinking matters more than acting. We found our own way through the crisis of the 1970s. Consultants are there to get your own ideas well presented or to do dirty work in a clean and polished style. We bring in technical advice from outside, and we go and look round our competitors.

5.   Ideally, innovation flows like a stream. In reality, it's a tough job. In our business, investment decisions are politically sensitive, often linked to regional policies. Our organization is changing

continuously, and with the minimum of formalities. The true organization chart is best kept in a locked drawer or, better still, in the managers' minds.

6.    In stormy weather, we've learned that a powerful captain is essential. A committee can lose the ship. But he must be sensitive to signals; otherwise, you end up going full speed in the wrong direction.

7.    Spaniards hate being told what to do. As a people, we're the opposite of the Japanese – each person thinks he's a leader. The only way to get acceptance is to explain the reasons why you want something done.

     Different leadership styles fit different levels in the company. Near the top, the rule is (c) – set the goals and let people reach them in their own way. In the middle, leadership is closely linked to training and coaching, so it's (a). On or near the factory floor, it's (b): the leader has to be physically close to the team and involved with them in detail. To summarize: at the top, the question is where to go; in the middle, it's where to go and how to get there; at the bottom it's how to get there.

8.    Human relations are good because we tell the truth. And the truth has to be clear and understandable. For example, the rule-book requires us to distribute our balance-sheet. But I know there's little point. I'm happy to hand it to an economist, because he'll understand it. If I give it to everyone, they'll just think I'm trying to confuse them.

     We used to play football with the workers, but I nearly got my leg broken, so I said 'Forget it. If you've got a grievance, bring it to me in my office. Don't kick my shins.'

     One thing which I'm especially proud of – well, I thank God who made me excellent! – is our special open day. Heavy industry in Spain is very divided on sex lines: work is for the man, home is for the woman. We open up one day per year to the wives and children, so they can see what their their husbands and fathers are doing, how the factory works, what the end product is. That makes them proud – and the fathers, too. Spanish pride may be a fault or a virtue, but management has to address it.

9.    Most of our output goes to Spanish industry, but our customers may well ship our stuff to their other factories in Germany or France. We also supply direct to other countries in the EC. Do we still call that export? I'm not so sure.

10.    Everyone on the payroll is Spanish.

**Respondent D: Scientist reporting to top management in a German pharmaceutical firm.**

1.      New conditions call for a new kind of manager. Change is now so rapid and unpredictable, both in our markets and in the political scene which shapes them. Traditionally, the German manager, especially in scientific fields, has been a planner; he works in a regulatory environment which encourages him to play safe. But the new manager must be able to cope with the unpredictable, with 'chaos', with creativity. We've been putting a lot of thought into this just recently: systems have to be there, but the client is the motor.

    Personnel work is very decentralized. Each manager is largely responsible for his own team, for recruiting and developing the right people.

3.      PR is an emotional area. We've gone in for a new corporate iden-tity package – logo and so on – but we find we have to do more these days. Social pressures, especially the environment issue, mean that quality and know-how no longer speak for themselves.

4.      We don't have the pyramid organization you'll find in larger Ger-man companies. Teamwork is the way. But who can you hang if things go wrong? We're always balancing between accountability on the one hand and freedom to take risks on the other.

5.      Innovation is our life-blood. Twenty-five per cent of turnover goes into R & D. It's a challenge, but not because of complacency. It takes eight years or more to develop a new drug; then we have a 10-year pay-back period in the market before the patent runs out. So we're under constant pressure, not only to find the new products, but to work more swiftly and to anticipate the market of the future.

6.      The team approach includes the top management. Bottom-up communication is easy and most new proposals start from below. But it could change: in times of crisis, you need a strong leader – just as the Romans used to appoint a dictator for war.

7.      Expertise is respected, because of the business we're in, and the right knowledge can outweigh rank. For example, I have to make an evaluation: should the company enter a certain new field? While it's going on, it's completely confidential to me and my team. No big boss can come and ask for details (once some-thing escaped, you'd never get the genie back in the bottle). When I present my conclusions, the boss might have been think-

ing 'Yes', but I'm saying 'No'. There'd be some discussion, a post-ponement to save the boss's face, but the final decision would be 'No'.

8.    During working hours, social contact is pretty relaxed. We all eat in the same canteen. Outside work, just where friendships happen to spring up – not a great deal between different levels.

9/10.    It's a private company with world-wide sales. Marketing offices are in perhaps 100 countries, but full-blown subsidiaries are only in a few key markets. Those are managed by locals. At heart it's a German company. You won't see many foreign faces at HQ canteen.

---

**Respondent E: Personnel manager in a major Japanese utility company.**

1.    We're very people-oriented. Subordinates do feel that their bosses trust them, that good performance will be seen and lead to promotion. The seniority system in Japanese companies means everyone can expect promotion, even automatic promotion, up to a certain level. But the road to the very top is only for the very few. Only the real profit producers will get there. Everyone has the dream that it could be him. The automatic promotion system encourages that dream, makes us all work harder, even in unsatisfactory working conditions. This is true of almost all big Japanese companies.

2.    Job definitions are very loose. The Japanese way is to hire the person, then train them as needed for the jobs that arise. The Western way is rather to define the job and then hire a person to fit it. In Japan we look for general talent with plenty of job rotation and training to prepare people for more senior posts.

3.    We've invested heavily in making our name known. We can say that it's been successful, but there is still some question as to whether the expenditure was really worthwhile.

4.    Consultation is very important to our decision-making, with plenty of face-to-face, one-to-one contact. During this stage decisions can be quite tough. Once consensus is reached, there is a meeting to announce it, which is just a formality.

5.    Innovation is natural. Shareholder pressure forces us to keep our customers happy and that means constantly bringing in new ideas.

6.     It's a group approach at the top and, as in all big companies, there's a risk of bureaucracy. In fact they're becoming more open to signals.

7.     Teamwork is the rule. Contact with my immediate superior is frequent, though never familiar. The one above him, I hardly contact at all.

8.     We go drinking together in the evening and when we run out of business topics we'll chat about sport, hobbies, family – but wives never appear. Home entertaining is difficult: Japanese homes are far from work and rather small. I might get invited to my boss's home once a year at most.

9/10.     As we are a utility, international steps are limited – by the nature of the business and by law. Even so, we send a dozen or so people each year to the US and Europe for education and training.

## In conclusion

Corporate culture, and the analysis of it, has been much in fashion in recent years. Currently on the market are a range of detailed diagnostics, enabling you to map every twist in your corporate nature. Our aim is simpler. The 10 points in the questionnaire should start to clarify your thoughts about your own company. More important is to start thinking about your partner's company: how do *they* make decisions? What kind of deals and relationships will attract *them*? What style of communication will they best understand?

---

**THE CULTURES OF GANGSTERISM**

The 1989 thriller *Black Rain* portrayed the misadventures of an American cop taking on Japanese mobsters (*yakuza*) on their home territory. The bullets do the same job, but the triggers are pulled for different reasons. Our hero needs a local cop to help him understand the motivations of the criminals.

> The yakuza gives Japan's no-hopers a role, a uniform, a lapel badge, a company song, an in-house magazine, and a relationship of childlike dependency to the Boss. It gives them, in Japanese terms, a life. For what is life without these things?
>
> The *Independent*, 3 February 1990

A British release, *The Krays*, shows an American criminal bigshot paying a business visit to his London counterparts, the Krays, whose welcome gift to him is a photograph of themselves with

---

their loving family – a recognition on their part of the 'family' nature of organized crime in America.

Another film, *The Long Good Friday* details the clash between a London gangster and the IRA, who are moving in on his territory. Their hard-bitten ideological motivations puzzle him; trying to deal with them according to his own 'ethics' gets him into deadly trouble.

In *The Godfather*, the chief adviser to generations of *mafiosi* is an *Irish* American, who acts as a bridge between the criminals and the Irish-dominated New York police department.

The criminal gangs of Moscow overlap with the local 'hooligans' and black marketeers, whose style and livelihood revolve around the scarce supply of fashionable Western goods.

The drug barons of Colombia and the Golden Triangle of South-East Asia rule in a style that local guerrilla leaders or warlords would recognize, and police methods for dealing with them are adapted accordingly.

The pickpocket gangs who roam Europe's shopping streets and sporting events are indistinguishable at airports from the tourists they prey on.

Next time you relax with a thriller, try to add something to your working model of the world's business cultures.

# EXERCISE

## *A LITTLE LIGHT READING*

Your company has a subsidiary in the imaginary land of Garundia, and you have been asked to go there for a two-week visit – 'Have a look around, get to know the people, come back and make proposals for improved communication.'

You know nothing about the place ('very valuable – look at the set-up through fresh eyes'), so you book a briefing session with George, an old Garundia hand, for the day before your departure. In preparation for that, you study last year's Report and Accounts from the Garundian subsidiary.

George goes sick. He telephones you: 'Don't worry about a thing. Lovely people, the Garundians. If you like, you can have a look around my office – pick up a little light reading for the flight . . .' (In case you didn't know, the flight to Garundia takes two-and-a-half hours, wherever in the world you start from.)

Below is a list of the items you find in George's rather chaotic office. Which would you put in your briefcase, and why?

1.  The 'Kings and Queens' volume from the 12-volume *Children's Encyclopedia Garundica*;

2.  your subsidiary's report and accounts from five years ago;

3.  a copy of George's entertainment expenses claim for his last visit to Garundia;

4.  last year's Report and Accounts from one of your local competitors in Garundia;

5.  *Explain me, Please!* – a Garundian phrase book;

6.  a Garundian cookbook, entitled *The Cuisine of a Cultural Crossroads*;

7.  an organization chart of your Garundian subsidiary, modified in pencil by George under the heading 'Who *really* does what';

8.  a road map of Garundia, incorporating a street map and public transport guide for the Garundian capital;

9.  a two-year-old *Financial Times* supplement on Garundia;

10. *The Lightning in Summer*, by Janko Torquinel – 'an action-packed historical romance set in the period of our country's birth';

11. a recent issue of *Deadline Garundin*, downloaded from the Internet 'showcasing all that is best in Garundian commerce and industry';

12. a catalogue, in Garundian, of your company's current products.

Try this exercise with a friend. If he has chosen the cookbook where you have chosen the *Financial Times*, you have learned something about each other's priorities.

There is no correct answer, but in Appendix 2A, at the end of this chapter, you will find a few of our thoughts on each of the 12 items.

## HUB, SPOKE AND RIM

> . . . we can have sympathy for the managing director of a newly acquired subsidiary . . . What is desperately needed is an account of how, whether and when the subsidiary *is* better off as part of a larger company than as an independent entity.
>
> Michael Goold and Andrew Campbell, *Strategies and Styles*

Different international and multinational companies distribute their internal power in different ways. Yet most executives working in most companies recognize the importance and difficulty of good communications between headquarters (the hub) and far-flung subsidiaries (along the spokes of the wheel). Even more problematic is an efficient system of communications from subsidiary to subsidiary (around the rim).

The HQ-based executive, with staff in a distant subsidiary reporting to him, cannot expect a creative attitude to communications around the rim unless he sets a good example himself in his dealings outward.

The 'corporate-seagull' is a well-established joke. He flies down from his elevated perch, deposits his message on those below, and flies away again. This section is addressed to the corporate seagull who would like to be more welcome on his next visit.

## A COSY PICTURE

Imagine yourself working on a fascinating project with a colleague of similar disposition, sharing the same office.

Now build in a little *motivation* problem: he ceases to pull his weight. That will change your relationship at least temporarily, but you have ample opportunity to talk it through with him and sort the problem out.

Next, promote one of you over the other, giving him the opportunity to pull rank at times of disagreement. Again, the relationship will be affected, causing as many ulcers in the new 'boss' as in the new 'subordinate'. Here you have problems of *hierarchy*.

So it might be time to move to separate offices. If you also regularly have lunch in the cafe on the corner while he uses the company canteen, you will be limiting *contact* to times when you have formal appointments. What are the effects on the working relationship?

Things are even more complicated if you vary the mix of *culture:* say you are a fourth generation Norwegian from the Bible Belt of the US, while she is a New Yorker from the Lower East Side.

These differences in background and outlook can be fruitful . . . with a bit of luck . . . always supposing you have a common *language* in which to discuss them. But if her first language is Spanish, while you failed first grade French at high school and gave up everything but English at that point?

Such are the overlapping issues in any act of communication between the head office controller and the local manager: motivation, hierarchy, contact, culture and language.

The degree to which a company has a genuinely international style often relates directly to how much the company sells outside the home market. The South American sales director of a Swiss pharmaceuticals company had previously worked for an American competitor.

> Of course my new company is more truly international. My former
> employers sold 80 per cent of their output within the US: American

research; American production and distribution, American con-
sumers. So they naturally exported their American management
style to deal with the other 20 per cent, and expected foreign
employees to conform to their ethics and practices. With the Swiss it's
a different story – and not only because they are naturally more cosmopolitan than the guys in New Jersey. They rotate jobs from country to country to help us learn each other's little ways, the company
newsletters are full of contributions fed through from local markets,
and conferences and seminars are a true two-way process. All this is
because they know they depend on us out here for survival: the Swiss
market is simply not big enough to recoup the terrifying research
and development costs. In fact, most of my job relates to these circumstances: I am a sort of Janus figure, with one face turned toward
Basel, explaining the South American scene in terms the HQ managers can understand, and the other face towards my Caribbean or
Inca sales force, interpreting for them the thought processes of the
alien Swiss and making them feel part of the family.

Let us leave the world of business for a while.

There is a clip of British War Office film from the early 1940s, showing
a wing of Hurricanes lining up on a wave of German bombers somewhere
over the North Sea. The soundtrack is synchronized from radio transmission, to give the full flavour of the event: you can actually hear what
the chaps were saying to each other over the ether as they went in.

The chaps were Polish – all except the Flight Officer, who was as English as they come. He was concerned that the radio channel be kept clear
for urgent warnings like 'Look out, Johnny! Bandit on your tail!'

English Flight Officer: 'Radio silence now. Good hunting.'

You need a Polish interpreter to make sense of what follows: an explo-
sion of bloodthirsty war-cries, boastful predictions of how many Jan is
going to shoot down, bets being placed, and disrespectful comments
about the long-haired English boy who seems to think he knows better
than seasoned pilots how to go into action. Radio silence it is not.

Nevertheless, the British/Polish team did well in the Battle of Britain.
Their objectives were clear, the enemy was visible, the crowds were cheer-
ing.

Under pressure like that, the barriers to international teamwork crum-
ble – while the battle is on, at least.

All the issues are there in that airborne example. In some areas, circumstances made a plus for the team, in others a minus.

● **Issue 1: Motivation**
   All the fighter pilots shared the same goals: to knock down a Dornier
   or two and return safe to base. Any individual who did not have these
   goals clearly in mind would soon find himself grounded. PLUS for
   team spirit.

- **Issue 2: Hierarchy**
  The 'boss' was flying the same machine, facing the same dangers. The derision he faced from the rest of the team was conventional and healthy – not to be compared with the hatred servicemen under fire feel for the staff tucked safely away behind the lines, or on the ground. PLUS, on the whole.

- **Issue 3: Contact**
  The infantry lieutenant in the field can use his charisma (or his revolver) to maintain discipline. In his cockpit above the clouds, the Flight Officer was a bit cut off. MINUS for our flying team.

- **Issue 4: Culture**
  Eton is a long way from Warsaw. But the working cultures had a lot in common: a fighter pilot is a fighter pilot the world over. PLUS in the air, potentially MINUS around the piano in the officers' mess.

- **Issue 5: Language**
  It is amusing to reflect that some of those Poles will have learnt 'wizard prang' or 'the magneto's knackered' (the jargon of the job) before they mastered the basics of English grammar. Certainly the ironic inflections of upper-class officers or Cockney ground crew will have meant little to them. MINUS overall for the team: the men doing the real job were largely cut off from their tactical decision maker, and from those providing the resources.

Having demonstrated how the five-issue analysis works, let us consider a more down-to-earth example, in the form of a short business case study.

## CASE STUDY

You are a Swede in the Stockholm head office of a company producing and marketing equipment for the world hospital market. Your company took over a big US competitor two years ago, for market share to absorb the output of your new robotized plant in Germany. Your board decided to clean out the US management team, but kept on the marketing director, Lou Salkin, now general manager of the US subsidiary. You got your MBA three years ago, while Lou has just quit tennis because of arthritis.

Lou asks you to speak to his salespeople at their annual conference, because he has noticed that they persist in referring to the company and its products by the name of ACME – the company's name before the takeover. The salespeople, by the way, are making better money than they were before.

**How will the encounter break down into the five categories?**

Not such a nightmare as it seems at first glance:

- Very little *language* gap (if you are like any Swedish business person we have ever met);

- *Culture* is not too remote (some Americans might not quite know where Sweden is, but you have been watching American TV programmes all your life) – but don't use too much of that MBA stuff in your presentation;

- Be direct on *hierarchy* (they will be on the lookout for signs of weakness);

- Seize this as a golden opportunity in terms of *contact*, and invite yourself to go out on the road with one of them for a day or two;

- Leave the issue of *motivation* to Lou – and that will motivate him. (You might suggest they hold their next annual conference on Swedish soil, if they hit their targets.)

Now what happens if we change the formula?

- Instead of the US, set the scene in your Benelux/Low Countries subsidiary. As a Swede, you are unlikely to be fluent in French, let alone Flemish. English is probably the best choice – but you will have to control it carefully: you are more accomplished in English than most Walloons. And you will have to keep checking that you have really understood what the Walloon is saying. *Language* problems will affect the result: it is difficult to transmit a subtle message with crude vocabulary, or through an interpreter.

- Instead of a flying visit, make it a two-year secondment: the nature of the *contact* changes. Now you have to make your tactical decisions, and shape your early messages, as a preparation for a set of relationships, rather than aiming simply for initial impact.

- You are a junior staff person from HQ addressing the local board: issues of *hierarchy* become more delicate.

- Your audience is drawn from both sides of the Belgian Flemish-Walloon divide, with some real Dutch and Luxembourgeois thrown in: you are no longer on a level playing field in terms of *culture*. Should you try to cater for the internal tensions?

- And finally, you have personal doubts about the message you have been asked to deliver. Perhaps the subsidiary would be better off going its own sweet way without interference. What happens to your *motivation*, and how well placed are you to motivate others?

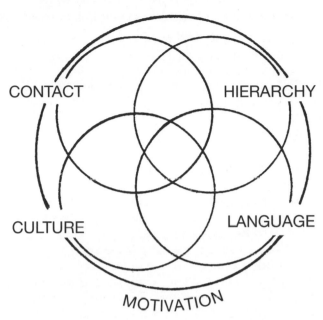

CONTACT         HIERARCHY

CULTURE        LANGUAGE

MOTIVATION

In the diagram above, motivation embraces all the other circles. This can be interpreted in two ways:

● That mutual motivation between the head office type and his counterpart in the foreign subsidiary can only flourish when the other four factors have been put in order and are running smoothly

● That somebody somewhere had better find the motivation to make sure that the other four factors *are* put in order and *do* run smoothly. (This is typically the job of the human resources/information specialist. The HRD man's role changes dramatically once a company goes international.)

We will now build that diagram, circle by circle, paying particular attention to the areas where the circles overlap.

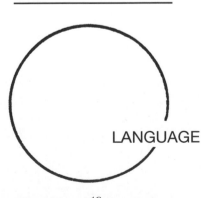

LANGUAGE

Let us consider an international conference, within a multinational company.

The delegates seated around the table are national representatives from Italy, France, Brazil, Venezuela, Germany, the US, Singapore, Japan, UK, Sweden . . . The language in use will certainly be English.

Now the question: of those listed, who has the trickiest problem as a communicator?

Answer: the American and the Briton, probably.

So long as the conversation is limited to practical business matters, there will be an unspoken agreement among the others to conduct the meeting in a simplified, general-purpose version of English. In its fully-fledged idiomatic form, English is notoriously difficult to handle, and most non-native speakers settle for a rudimentary version: a tool to get the job done.

An insider, who has grown up speaking some version of 'real' English without thinking, finds it difficult to step down from his lofty perch and make his points with simplified syntax, controlled idiom and vocabulary. When he does try to make adjustments, the result is usually clumsy and ineffectual – embarrassed and embarrassing, in fact.

Here is a true story to illustrate the need.

Civil aircraft manufacturers run highly sophisticated sales operations, which place great emphasis on good client relations. After all, there are only so many airlines in the world to buy the machines they make. One manufacturer we know well employs several nationalities in its sales/technical support functions, and English is the company language – both inside, and in communication with most of its customers.

Recently, a South-East Asian client introduced a new condition for future dealings: they were happy to communicate in English, as all their key employees were competent, but would the manufacturer please ensure that from now on no native speakers of English were involved? They were too hard to understand, and apparently had difficulty in understanding what was said to them . . .

Chapter 6 is largely devoted to describing this phenomenon, and suggesting practical ways around it. We have called the language for international use 'Offshore English'.

---

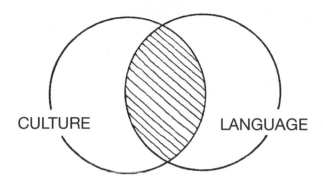

CULTURE       LANGUAGE

Culture was our concern in Chapter 1.

We hope that you already see the value of *facts/attitudes/behaviour* model building, described in Chapter 1 as a more coherent approach than the random accumulation of cross-cultural tips and hints.

Our corporate seagull must also pay attention to the attitudes that go with given functions in a corporation. When we have written case studies for management trainees, we have often sought a universal conflict which they would all recognize. To make the case study go with a swing, the trick is to exaggerate the conflict: salesmen on the road think that marketing men are airy-fairy and detached from reality; both groups suspect the production manager of obstructiveness, while he thinks they only exist to disrupt his carefully-laid production plans; the financial controller believes that the company exists to balance its books, and is seen by everybody else as a secret policeman; the training manager in HRD has the company's future in the palm of his hand, but has great difficulty seducing people away from their desks to attend vital training courses.

Of course, in a well-ordered company, such clashes of interest should be a thing of the past, but when you are an outsider on a visit, it is wise to assume that they are still there. People love to form armed camps. Never plan on the basis that the people in the subsidiary are all one happy family, even if they try to give you that impression.

---

**The way a culture speaks**

We were present recently at a strategy planning session in Eastern Europe. The event was to be spread over a weekend, and conducted in English and Hungarian simultaneously – through a relaxed system of interpreting that would ensure nobody felt left out.

The first job to be done – and it was taken very seriously – was to reach agreement on the form of address appropriate to the weekend. First-name familiarity was natural to the Americans and British present, whose average age was in the early 30s. The Hungarian contingent included several rather older members, who seemed likely to stand on their dignity. The chairman addressed them first, and asked their permission for first names and familiar grammar (*te* rather than *ön* – a subtlety that does not occur in English, since the death of the *thou/you* distinction). This was not just a formality: the older generation consulted each other with raised eyebrows and agreed with nods. 'Good,' sighed the chairman, 'it is done.'

Soon afterwards, one of the Hungarians expressed regret that 'cliques' had been forming in the offices. The Americans shrugged it off – it always happens, and who cares anyway? The Hungarians closed ranks: *they* cared. A lot of fuss about nothing? We asked the two groups to give us their associations around the word 'clique'. The Americans offered 'tennis, parties, fun, gossip' and the Hungarians 'conspiracy, power-seeking, wickedness, dictatorship'.

Look for associations and connotations. Do not trust the first definition you find in a dictionary.

> We dissect nature along lines laid down by our native languages.
> Benjamin Lee Whorf, linguist

Language is not only what you speak in. Much deeper than that, it is what you think with – you cannot think about something you cannot name.

**The way a culture thinks**

Here we touch on a difference in patterns of thought and styles of argument which we have often seen create tension. When a representative of Culture A tells his Culture B partner 'You are not being logical', he usually means 'You are approaching this issue in an unfamiliar, disturbing way'.

The form of reasoning instilled in Northern European secondary school children goes like this: examine all the evidence, try to detect a pattern, form a general rule to cover all cases, subject your newly-formed rule to rigorous testing. If it survives, you have your theory, policy or proposal. If not, you have learned a great deal during the process. So a good teacher spends a long time exercising his pupils' minds *before* giving them the answer. In subjects like literature and history, there is often no answer.

In Southern Europe, and in Catholic enclaves further north, educational systems are often still redolent of the catechism: 'Who made the world?' 'God made the world' – and everything follows from that. The 17th-century philosopher, Descartes, started his approach to the truth by clearing his mind of all but one undeniable statement: 'I think, therefore I am.' On that he built his system. Descartes is still a powerful influence on the French way of thinking.

> Much of the best and worst in the French national spirit can be imputed to this concept of education as inspired academic pedagogy confined to the classroom walls: its role is to transmit knowledge and to train intellects, not – as in Britain – to develop the full individual.
>
> John Ardagh, *France in the 1980s*

Two sets of factors emerge:

| **A** | **B** |
| --- | --- |
| Northern Europe | Southern Europe |
| Protestant | Catholic |
| Germanic/Anglo-Saxon | Latin |
| Education = Development | Education = Instruction |
| Loose school curricula | Centralized curriculum |
| Experience has value | Qualifications have value |

A person from a background scoring five out of six in Column A is likely to approach any given problem differently to a Column B type.

So when Lars Svensson tries to persuade Jean-Marie Dupont to his point of view, all his background culture is pushing him to begin from the basic known facts and work up: 'As you know, 80 per cent of our customers are regular buyers. We've got an 11 per cent market share. Inflation is dropping. And there are several other factors we should consider before we start to explore the various avenues that are open to us . . .'

Jean-Marie has his teeth clenched. He wants to hear Lars' proposal upfront, so that they can do as he was taught at school, and seek evidence in support of that proposal. He feels that the man from headquarters is patronizing him by stating the obvious, and exhibits his natural impatience: 'Yes, yes. I see all that, of course! The best approach is obviously to . . .'

'So irrational, so impatient, so Latin!', thinks Lars.

'So pedestrian, so cold, so Northern!', thinks Jean-Marie.

To sum up:

- Column A cultures tend to present like this: 'The facts are; . . . and these are the most relevant facts; . . . so we can see various ways forward . . ., of which *this* is the best; . . .'

- Column B cultures tend to present arguments as follows: '*This* is the best way forward because . . . and because . . . and because . . . and here are some more underlying facts; . . .'

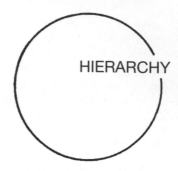

For our corporate seagull, the important thing to remember is that there are mutually antagonistic mind-sets in head office and in the subsidiary. Subsidiary perceives HQ as bureaucratic, academic, and overstaffed with patricians reclining on couches eating grapes. Meanwhile HQ views subsidiary as short-sighted, ignorant of the broad view, suspicious of new initiatives and prone to making promises they have no intention of keeping.

We bring these tensions to the surface on management training courses with a simple jigsaw puzzle. Two teams are told that they are managers (M) and workers (W) respectively. The M team are told to brief the W team to assemble the pieces of the puzzle. They immediately assume that the W team will not be bright enough to work it out for themselves, and spend an inordinate amount of time planning, drafting step-by-step instructions, and guarding the door of the M room against intrusion. The W team spends a corresponding period waiting for information, building up resentment, and probably planning a strike. The referees have to be alert: long-standing relationships can be damaged when a W realizes that his old friend only has to become an M in order to treat him like a fool.

We have found this hierarchical stereotype to be even stronger than ethnic or geographical distinctions. All acts of communication along the spokes of the wheel take place against this background of suspicion.

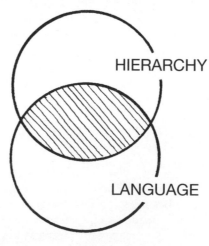

Here is a tip for Lars (from HQ), when he has an idea to get across to Jean-Marie (subsidiary). Don't say '*We* think you can tighten your belts in the third quarter of the financial year', say rather '*I* think you can etc, etc'. If the man from the subsidiary hears that 'we' form, he perceives a *fait accompli* imposed by a faceless gang who have little idea of what it means to make a living in the real world. He might even suspect that you personally have doubts about the validity of the statement. Using 'I' leaves the way open for true person-to-person dealing, and reserves the 'we' to represent Lars plus Jean-Marie – the team who will solve the problem together.

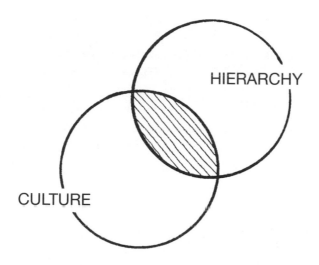

The official organization chart in your subsidiary probably reflects the corporate view on how things should be run. It does not necessarily match the feelings of the people on the ground. Those feelings grow, in large measure, out of the local country culture.

How likely is that culture to see a command structure as an inverted pyramid, with the bosses supporting the people who are doing the real work?

On some organization charts today, we find top management in the left-hand margin, with salaries decreasing as we read from left to right – a compromise, perhaps, but an indication that the company is not run on strictly top-down principles.

The seagull has to modify his style when the laws of gravity are changed.

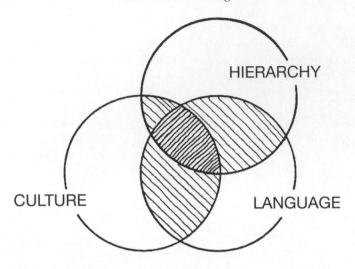

Here is a true story to sum this up, and again it involves Lars and Jean-Marie:

The Frenchman had been working for the Swedes for three years, and it was a good deal: he was running one of their French subsidiaries, hitting his targets, getting on well with his staff, using his local knowledge to effect improvements in distribution. Yet he didn't feel trusted, somehow, by HQ in Gothenburg. They always looked at him a bit critically during meetings. He took it up with Lars.

'Tell me, Jean-Marie – yes, I will have a little more wine – when was the last time you had this feeling?'

'Well, for example, at this year's budget conference in January. It all went smoothly for a day-and-a-half, there seemed to be a general meeting of minds. And yet . . .'

'What actually happened? Who said what?'

'The chairman asked me formally if I was prepared to commit myself to this very tough budget.'

'And what did you say?'

'Well naturally I said 'Why not?'' (Accompanying this with an enormous Gallic shrug . . .)

When a Swede asks you earnestly to commit yourself to an earnest business proposition, he wants a level gaze, and no hint of irony or light-heartedness. When a Frenchman is asked if he can take a machine-gun nest single-handed, his self-image demands that he deliver that existential shrug, stub out an imaginary Gauloise, and go over the top with a grin.

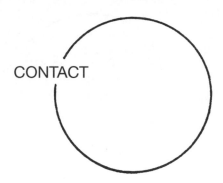

CONTACT

In our original ideal picture at the beginning of this section (cosy team-work with no complicating factors), you had plenty of opportunity for informal contact with that colleague in the same office.

If your partner is a long way away you have to *plan* for contact. We have collected tips from experienced international managers on how to do this planning. Here are a few of our favourites:

- I try to visit each of my subsidiaries four times a year:
  - budget;
  - budget review;
  - let's clear the desk of paperwork and talk blue skies;
  - I understand the salmon fishing is good at this time of year.
                              General manager, toiletries firm

- Whether the visit is four hours or three days, I always devote the first 51 per cent of the agenda to local problems. I listen, offer sympathy and advice if appropriate. Then and only then do I start talking about corporate objectives and the local contribution. The managers down there are in no mood to listen to what I have to say until they've got their worries off their chests.
                    Senior partner, international consultancy group

- Even when you think they've got the idea, put in a call a few days after you've left, just to check. Find a pretext – 'I've lost my notes of the meeting' will do – and ask them to give their version of what was agreed. You'll be amazed at the distortions that can creep in.
                    Desk manager for Western Europe, American
                              light engineering group

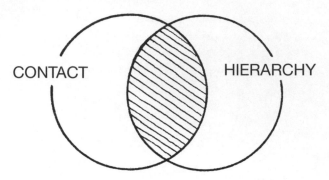

There is a delicate balance to be struck between taking an interest in what subordinates are doing, and breathing down their necks. Nothing is more demotivating than to have the boss, on a flying visit, tampering with systems you have developed and which produce excellent results.

Picture a kitchen where one partner is cooking, from instinct and years of practice, a dish that has never failed to please. The other appears with a cookery book open at the relevant page and begins to offer constructive criticism . . .

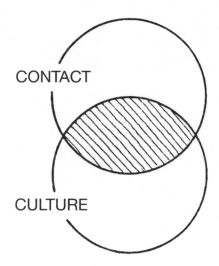

There is a close correspondence between the subordinate's tolerance of interference and his sense of personal space.

In cultures where men walk arm-in-arm along the street, there is a greater readiness to accept guidance at close quarters – provided it is delivered with due regard for all the other factors in the relationship.

In regions where people seldom touch more closely than an arm's-length handshake, it is better not to interfere unless invited.

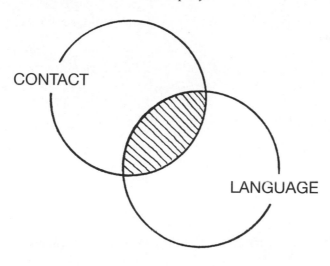

I have a million ideas and only five hundred English words.
Senior engineer, Italian tyre company

If your command of English-as-lingua franca is good, please be considerate of those who are only just surviving. We have seen stress build up to the point of tears in big strong men who have been forced to sit through four-hour meetings, concentrating not only on the business in hand, but on following the language and formulating their ideas fast enough to contribute.

Call frequent breaks for their sake. In terms of the quality of information exchanged and ideas generated, it will be more efficient than just going on and on.

If, on the other hand, you are the sufferer, don't be afraid to ask for a short break – perhaps to discuss the last agenda point with colleagues in your own language, to make sure you have things clear.

### A FINAL ANECDOTE

Getting things clear was Lars's job. Equipped with his MBA, he was despatched by headquarters to tour the subsidiaries, meet the people, and gather data for the new five-year sales plan in the power generation division. The French subsidiary, recently acquired, was operating a policy of disinformation. The chief executive officer felt that the best way to preserve autonomy was to keep HQ in the dark. The figure he gave to Lars was deliberately distorted.

The British manager felt it would be unkind to deliver his usual line on forecasts ('We're not selling knives and forks! How can you have a forecast for power stations?'). Instead, he took Lars for a long lunch, gossiped for a while about HQ politics, and gave him a gently pessimistic figure to put in his briefcase.

The Italian explained how different things always are in Italy – fragmented market, everything depending on a network of contacts, how the time he was spending with Lars would have been better spent cultivating those contacts . . . and gave him a random figure to play with.

The German provided a ring-bound volume full of calculations, based on interlocking best-case/worst-case analyses, predictions of D-Mark fluctuations, and statistical breakdowns of the competition's performance over the last 20 years.

The American leaned over the table, bared his teeth, and said: 'My forecast? I'll give you my forecast . . . We're gonna win!'

Lars returned to HQ, cooked all the data he had collected in his stop, and produced a curve.

He gave it to the chief executive officer, who hung it on his office wall.

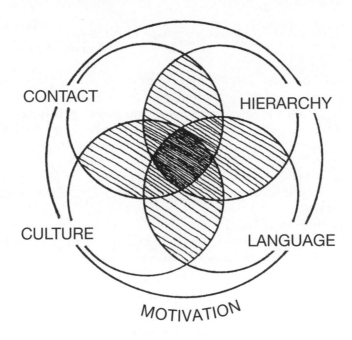

# APPENDIX 2A – NOTES ON 'A LITTLE LIGHT READING'

Here are just a few thoughts on the usefulness or otherwise of what you found in George's office.

1. *Children's Encyclopedia Garundica* – 'Kings and Queens' volume
   This might be a bit heavy – in both senses. That said, it is probably a better bet than the adult version. Serious reference books are full of detail that is difficult to absorb, while 'Did You Know?' books can be quite accurate yet digestible.
   The information itself will probably have little bearing on your business in Garundia, but it can score big points if you are able to point at the statue in the market-place and say: 'Ah, yes, that's Stig the Liberator, isn't it?'

2. Report and Accounts from five years ago
   You have already studied last year's, we said. By comparing the two, you might detect some rough financial trends, and determine how many promises the CEO has been keeping.

3. George's expenses claim
   Might give you some insight into levels and costs of entertaining in Garundia. It depends on how scrupulously George plays the game.

4. Competitor's report and accounts
   Could be useful if you know how Garundians lay out their accounts. Or if you want to learn.

5. Phrase book
   Definitely a good idea to learn a few words of greeting on the plane.

6. Cookbook
   Some material for small talk, perhaps, but the contents may bear little resemblance to what is served in the average restaurant or canteen.

7. Annotated organization chart
   Potentially useful item. George's notes might not be totally objective, of course, but properly handled, they will give you a flying start. People and their real concerns are the reason you are getting on the plane.

8. Map
   Any map can tell you a great deal about a place (see Chapter 1), besides helping you find your way around.

9. Old *Financial Times* supplement
Very useful, though going out of date. At that age, *The Economist* equivalent would be more valuable, giving a longer-term view.

10. Historical romance
Read a few paragraphs: a pleasant way to take in a lot of cultural background, or a monumental bore? Make a note of author and title – Torquinel might be a national hero, and you might find yourself addressing a chamber of commerce conference in the Torquinel suite of the local Hilton.

11. Internet print-out
Probably dull, possibly distorted, but another source of useful names.

12. Product catalogue
Useful for picking up some vocabulary related to your field – which won't be in the phrasebook.

# 3

# Character

Your business partner is more than his company's delegate or mouthpiece. He is a human being, with standards, drives and moods. The human relationship is crucial to good business.

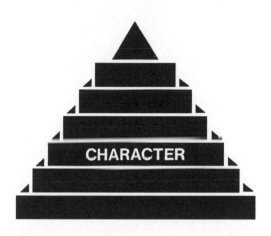

Ten lands are more easily known than one man
Yiddish proverb

At the end of Chapter 1, we encouraged you to start developing a flexible model of the culture from which your business partner springs. We also pointed out the need to be alert to deviations from the norms that make up your model. The deviations you encounter will often be an expression of individual character traits; it is important not to let your expectations of, say, Chinese behaviour blind you to the behaviour patterns of the particular Chinese you are dealing with.

It is this individual character who should be hearing your message, buying your product, supporting you in the team. You can only improve your chances if you take steps to shape your arguments to appeal to this individual – your partner. Where is he starting from? Where is he going? What does he know? What does he want?

# DIG A BIT DEEPER

We are all deeply aware of social taboos, including the rule against probing too deeply into other's feelings. And when we are among strangers, it is particularly easy to get things wrong.

> I started conversation with the men opposite [on a train in China] . . .
> They turned out to be professional painters and administrators in an art museum, but when I asked one about his feelings for landscape, I realised that I'd gone too far. His gaze detached itself, his smile expanded, and he said nothing. But the official beside him looked appalled, and whispered across to me: 'Mr Kung is now Deputy Director of our museum. You cannot ask such personal things' . . .
>
> Colin Thubron, *Behind the Wall*

On the other hand:

> I was at a reception during my first business trip to China, and making conversation with a member of the host delegation. I don't know why, but I suddenly wanted to know something about him personally. It spilled out: 'What happened to you during the Cultural Revolution?'
>
> He became very excited, called for everybody's attention, and made an announcement in Mandarin, very heated, gesturing towards me. I could see from his colleagues' reaction that they were shocked, and I wanted the ground to open up and swallow me. They gathered in a huddle, gesticulating earnestly and ignoring me completely.
>
> I turned in despair to a more experienced colleague, who understood Mandarin. He was very reassuring: 'Disaster? Quite the opposite. They might never have found a way of raising the subject among themselves, although the Cultural Revolution was the biggest event by far in so many lives. Now they're having a real conversation about it, and all thanks to you.'
>
> French civil engineer

This was more by luck than judgement, of course. But if you take no risks in this area, you have no chance at all of getting lucky.

Try looking at it this way: being a stranger to local customs means either walking in fear of getting things wrong, and so doing nothing, or using your forgivable ignorance as a licence to dig a bit deeper. In this chapter we will be suggesting how to do that digging.

Our suggestions are chiefly in the form of questions. As your working relationship with a given partner develops, these are some of the questions to which you should be finding answers.

## QUESTION: IS THERE SOME DEEP GENERAL PRINCIPLE MY PARTNER IS APPLYING?

According to researchers at Ohio State University, all human behaviour can be boiled down to 15 desires and values. Only three of those are shaped by our upbringing; the rest are genetic.

Influenced by upbringing:

- *Citizenship*: the desire for public service.

- *Independence*: the desire to make one's own decisions.

- *Rejection*: the fear of social isolation.

Built in genetically:

- *Curiosity*: the desire to learn.

- *Hunger*: the desire to eat.

- *Honour*: the desire to behave in accordance with a code of conduct.

- *Sex*: the desire for sexual behaviour and fantasies.

- *Physical exercise*: the desire for physical activity.

- *Order*: the desire for organization in daily life.

- *Vengeance:* the desire to retaliate when offended.

- *Social contact:* the desire to be in the company of others.

- *Family:* the desire to spend time with one's own relations.

- *Social prestige:* the desire for position and positive attention.

- *Aversive sensations:* aversion to pain and anxiety.

- *Power:* the desire to influence people.

Business is business the world over, of course, But often there is some other strong drive behind your partner – a more or less atavistic force that he might hardly be conscious of. The force could derive from the local background culture, or else from the principles of the organization he works for. (Many companies these days have enshrined values: 'Dedication; Teamwork; Decisiveness; Excellence.')

A good way to start exploring Character is by testing responses to proverbs. We often use the following short questionnaire as the starting point for a discussion on this theme.

Try it on yourself, then turn to Appendix 3A, at the end of this chapter, where we provide some results from a variety of nationalities.

**Proverbs questionnaire**

Look at the following proverbs and sayings. How central are the points they make to the way you run your life, both business and personal? Give a mark on the scale from 0 = Irrelevant, to 8 = Essential.

'Time is money'
0  1  2  3  4  5  6  7  8

'Blood is thicker than water'
0  1  2  3  4  5  6  7  8

'My word is my bond'
0  1  2  3  4  5  6  7  8

God will provide'
0  1  2  3  4  5  6  7  8

'Do as you would be done by'
0  1  2  3  4  5  6  7  8

## QUESTION: HOW NORMAL A PRODUCT OF HIS CULTURAL BACKGROUND IS MY PARTNER? AND HOW TYPICAL OF HIS COMPANY?

Having developed your model of your partner's way of life, and having studied the values of his organization, you now have a reference point against which to measure your partner:

● He seems to be a stickler for detail, but is he exceptionally so, given his background?

● He avoids committing himself on paper whenever he can. Is this unusual?

● He never stops singing his company's praises. Is he just part of the chorus?

## QUESTION: WHAT CONTRADICTION IN HIMSELF IS MY PARTNER TRYING TO RESOLVE?

> Do I contradict myself?
> Very well then I contradict myself
> (I am large, I contain multitudes).
> Walt Whitman

Classical drama, from ancient Greece to 17th-century France, depended on the resolution of conflicts – the struggle of a tragic king between his patriotic duty and his passion for an enemy queen; the disputes among courtiers over the 'civilized' values of the town versus the 'natural' values of the countryside.

More recently, Jung, the Swiss psychologist, suggested that beneath the level of daily thoughts, each unconscious mind is striving to resolve and balance countervailing forces – light/dark, masculine/feminine. His compatriot, the linguist Saussure, inspired the French anthropologist Lévi-Strauss in his development of *structuralism* in the 1960s. Until then anthropology had been primarily concerned with compiling ethnographic data – marriage customs in this nomadic tribe, coming-of-age rituals in that cluster of Pacific islands. Lévi-Strauss sought a universal system or model, based on a set of polarities – for example the distinction between those foods which are consumed raw and those which must be cooked.

This idea of polarities underlines the work of a series of 'culture gurus' active in management circles since the 1960s. The first was Edward Hall, an American who visited Europe to study the workings of managers in organizations.

## GURU 1: EDWARD HALL

In Hall's *The Silent Language*, there are two key concepts:

1. High Context vs Low Context

*High context* communicators suppose that the people they are talking to are wise to the context in which the message is set: my listeners have a good idea what this is all about, and if they don't know they can guess. So in high context cultures ideas are not spelt out in detail. People depend on each other to piece together the whole message within the context they both understand, and try not to bore each other with step-by-step explanations. Communication depends to a great extent on facial expressions, body language, inflexions of the voice and eye contact. Those raised in such an atmosphere can get impatient with low context communicators.

*Low context* communicators like to spell things out, and to have things spelt out to them. Sentences are completed. Only one person speaks at a time. Telephone agreements are confirmed by fax. These people sometimes think that high context communicators are chaotic, secretive, unreliable and emotional.

2. Polychronic vs Monochronic

In *polychronic* cultures, people answer the phone, drink coffee, transmit sign language to their colleagues, listen to your presentation, and think about lunch all at the same time. They get bored and restless if only one thing is happening.

In *monochronic* cultures, timetables are respected and activities are carefully compartmentalized.

Hall examines France and Northern Germany, and finds the French to be High Context/Polychronic, and the Germans to be Low Context/Monochronic. He also poses the question: if we study a large American business organization, which of the European cultures might we find? (To express the idea another way: as the waves of migrants crossed the Atlantic, which boat carried the cultural germ of IBM, General Motors, Coca-Cola?) The answer, Hall found, was simple: the manners and mores of office life in American business are essentially German.

## GURU 2: GEERT HOFSTEDE

Following Hall, there was a Dutch researcher, Geert Hofstede. His book *Culture's Consequences* is based on a large scale, rigorous survey of IBM subsidiaries: early 1970s, 116,000 questionnaires, 70+ countries. Each national culture scores high to low along four dimensions.

1. Power-Distance
In *high power-distance* cultures: the boss is the boss, everyone is in his place, employees are afraid to criticize (France, India). While by the *low power-distance* code superiors and subordinates are colleagues, those in power try to look less powerful than they are, employees expect to be consulted (Austria, Israel).

2. Uncertainty-Avoidance
Where *uncertainty-avoidance* is normal behaviour: people feel the need for clarity and order, they work hard in stable careers and abhor deviance, company rules are observed even when damage may result (Japan, Greece). While in countries where they don't 'avoid uncertainty' each day is taken as it comes, people take a pragmatic view of rules and regulations, people are more mobile from job to job (Denmark, Hong Kong).

3. Individualism
In highly *individualistic* cultures: the emphasis is on personal initiative and achievement the ideal is to be a good leader, everyone has the right to a private life and opinion (USA, Britain). While at the opposite pole of 'collectivism' loyalty to the clan is rewarded by the clan's protection, the ideal is to be a good member, commitment to the work organization overrides personal inclinations (Iran, Peru).

4. Masculinity
Natives of *high masculinity* cultures: have these values: performance counts – and is measured partly in material standards; ambition is the driving force; big and fast are beautiful and *machismo* is sexy (Australia, Italy). While at the 'feminine' end quality of life matters more than standard of living; service/people/the environment are the focus; small is beautiful and unisex is attractive (Netherlands, Sweden).

## GURU 3: FONS TROMPENAARS

Another Dutchman, Fons Trompenaars, took the same pattern of ideas further, casting his net wider and, some would say, bending the rules of statistical analysis as he tried to resolve paradoxes. For Europe, he confirmed Hall's groupings:

> All the examples show that there is a clear-cut cultural border between the North-West European (analysis, logic systems and rationality) and the Euro-Latin (more person-related, more use of intuition and sensitivity).

His polarities are expressed as scales, derived from the responses to key questions, most of which are to do with relationships between the individual and society.

Scale 1. Would you give evidence against a friend who had been speeding and caused a traffic accident? *Universalism* says good and bad can be defined for all circumstances; *particularism* gives greater attention to the obligations of relationships and unique situations.

Scale 2. Should the team take responsibility for a mistake made by one member? *Individualism* leaves people free to contribute to the collective as and if they wish; *collectivism* puts the emphasis on shared benefits and judges individuals by what they put in.

Scale 3. If you are upset at work, should you display your feelings? *Neutral* cultures spawn business relationships which are instrumental and focus on objectives; *emotional* business dealings – involving anger, joy and passion – are acceptable at the other end of the scale.

Scale 4. If your boss asked you to help paint his house, would you? *Specific* behaviour puts contractual before personal concerns; *diffuse* behaviour overlaps the two sets of issues, and takes time to weave them together.

Scale 5. In your culture, does the 'right' family name carry weight? *Achievement-oriented* attitudes judge you on what you have recently accomplished; *ascription-orientation* awards status according to birth, kinship, gender, age, connections, school, etc.

Trompenaars' other key observations concern attitudes to time and the environment.

- Time. Concentration on past accomplishments, or on plans for the future? The American Dream is the French Nightmare. Does time pass in a straight line, as a series of disparate events, or is it seen as a circle of present and past together with future possibilities?

● Environment. Do we derive our motivations and values from within ourselves and shape our world to suit us, or do the powers of nature, fate and history render our efforts puny? Is the Walkman to protect the world from our noise, or to protect our listening pleasure from the world's intrusion?

### *GURU 4: JOHN MOLE*

The idea of a cultural fault-line, running across Europe from North-East to South-West, is at the heart of John Mole's book *Mind Your Manners*, where we are given a generalized portrait of each of the 12 EC members (1993 edition). Then in the section on 'attitudes, values and beliefs', we have 'The Mole Map'. The key polarities are to do with Style of Leadership (Individual < > Group) and Style of Organization (Organic < > Systematic).

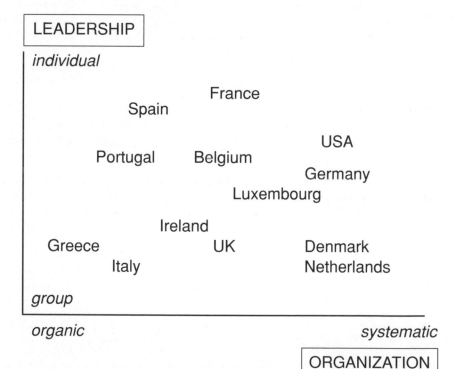

(If you spin this diagram through 180 degrees, you will find a more telling distribution with the 'hero cultures' in the South-East quadrant, and the 'consensus cultures' to the North-West.)

## GURU 5: RICHARD D LEWIS

In *When Cultures Collide*, Lewis compresses these polarities into a generalized checklist.

LINEAR-ACTIVE

1. Germans, Swiss

2. Americans (WASP)

3. Scandinavians, Austrians

4. British, Canadians, New Zealanders

5. Australians, South Africans

6. Japanese

7. Dutch, Belgians

8. American subcultures (eg, Jewish, Italian, Polish)

9. French, Belgians (Walloons)

10. Czechs, Slovenians, Croats, Hungarians

11. Northern Italians (Milan, Turin, Genoa)

12. Chileans

13. Russians, other Slavs

14. Portuguese

15. Polynesians

16. Spanish, Southern Italians, Mediterranean peoples

17. Indians, Pakistanis, etc

18. Latin Americans, Arabs, Africans

MULTI-ACTIVE

Introvert, patient, quiet, minds own business, likes privacy, plans ahead (methodically), does one thing at a time, works fixed hours, punctual, dominated by timetables and schedules, compartmentalizes projects, sticks to plans, sticks to facts, gets information from statistics/reference books/database, job-oriented, unemotional, works within department, follows correct procedures, accepts favours reluctantly, delegates to competent colleagues, completes action chains, likes fixed agendas, brief on telephone, uses memoranda, respects officialdom, dislikes losing face, confronts with logic, limited body language, rarely interrupts, separates social-professional.

Extrovert, impatient, talkative, inquisitive, gregarious, plans grand outline only, does several things at once, works any hours, unpunctual, timetable unpredictable, lets one project influence another, changes plans, juggles facts, gets first-hand (oral) information, people-oriented, emotional, gets round all departments, pulls strings, seeks favours, delegates to relations, completes human transactions, interrelates everything, talks for hours, rarely writes memos, seeks out (top) key person, has ready excuses, confronts emotionally, unrestricted body language, interrupts frequently, interweaves social/professional

Lewis provides a third dimension: REACTIVES – those cultures that prioritize courtesy and respect, listening quietly and calmly to their interlocutors and reacting carefully to the other side's proposals. Chinese, Japanese and Finns are in this group: introvert, patient, silent, respectful, good listener, looks at general principles, reacts, flexible hours, punctual, reacts to partner's timetable, sees whole picture, makes slight changes, statements are promises, people-oriented, quietly caring, all departments, inscrutable, calm, protects face of other, delegates to reliable people, reacts to partner, thoughtful, summarizes well, plans slowly, ultra honest, must not lose face, avoids confrontation, subtle body language, doesn't interrupt, connects social and professional.

We have included these synopses of the gurus' works in this chapter on Character because we believe that this is where most international business people find such ideas useful: If I am negotiating a contract with Mr Adamashvili; am I dealing with an average Georgian working in a normal Georgian way (very multi-active), or is this partner an exception – disciplining himself to be less polychronic when he does business with visitors from the North-West? If I make a High-Context remark – an oblique suggestion – to Miss Lindroos, will her Finnish mind grasp the idea, or should I spell it out a bit more clearly? The staff of our operation in Lyons seem to come up with more innovative ideas when their boss is out of the way. Is this a failing in Mr Avocat's leadership style, or just a typical French response to the presence of a hierarchical superior? This leads to the next of our key questions.

### QUESTION: IS MY PARTNER'S PERSONALITY INTEGRATED WITH HIS ORGANIZATION, OR IS HE WEARING A MASK?

Being employed in a corporation is a recent phenomenon – it's hardly natural at all. When we enter employment, we accept that our behaviour will be modified. The rules vary from job to job, employer to employer. The copywriter in the creative department of an advertising agency has greater latitude, traditionally, than the counter clerk in a high street bank, while the farm-hand can be freer than either.

A farm-hand who suddenly discovered a talent in himself for advertising slogans would have a hard time adjusting to the pace of life of Madison Avenue. If he survived for long enough, though, the demands on his behaviour would begin to affect his attitude.

We can show it diagrammatically like this:

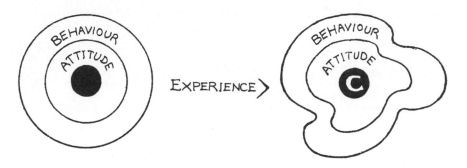

As the outer circle (Behaviour) is pushed and pulled into the shape a career requires, so the circle within (Attitude) flexes accordingly. If your job requires you to get up at 5.00 am – a change in behaviour – your attitude to bed changes too. If your attitude to your company's products is blocking your success as a salesman, you work on it, and the improvement shines through in your behaviour.

And the fixed ring in the middle? The one that does not change shape? Character.

In society at large, and in the workplace in particular, there are limits to how far Tom can make changes in Harry, how deeply he can cut with his criticizm. These limits are not always clearly defined, but crossing them is always deeply resented.

'Criticize what I *do*, but never what I *am*.'

The size of the Character circle in our diagram is arbitrary. Should it dominate the picture, suggesting that the Self is very powerful, wearing a veneer in the workplace? Or should it be a mere dot, suggesting that the Self is deeply hidden while its owner gets on with the vital jobs of earning a living, building a career, and generally fitting in?

Often, as people follow their career paths, they become more personally involved in their work. More and more they are what they do.

Of course, there are local variations:

> I have noticed that many of my British colleagues use what the Japanese call *tatemae*, or outside face. In general, the British tend to be more formal or diplomatic, while American tend to be more direct, emotive and explosive, showing the real face, or *honne*.
> An American management trainer working
> for a British company in Tokyo

## QUESTION: HOW IS MY PARTNER VIEWED BY HIS COLLEAGUES, OR HIS BOSS?

Make a deliberate effort to watch how your partner's team functions within itself. What is the pecking order? Where does he stand in it? How do his colleagues react when he makes a proposal? How formally do they address him?

Is he feared? Respected? Tolerated? Despised?

> There are four types of young officer. The stupid and lazy ones you can forget about: either the enemy or their own men will dispose of them. The intelligent and lazy will stay out of harm's way: pay them no attention. Then we have the intelligent, energetic type: beware, they want your position. Finally, there are the stupid, energetic ones: it is your job to take them out and shoot them before they ruin everything.
>
> Attributed to the Duke of Wellington

## QUESTION: WHAT SORT OF MOOD IS MY PARTNER IN? HOW IS HIS MIND WORKING?

As behavioural psychology has broadened and diversified, new tools have emerged.

Neuro Linguistic Programming (NLP) is such a tool. Put very simply, it divides mental activity into three types: visual, auditory and kinaesthetic.

Each person functions predominantly in one of these modes, switching to the others occasionally. *Eye movements* and *choice of idiom* provide the clues.

### Eye movements

The visual mode can be identified by eye movements in the upward direction, the auditory by horizontal and the kinaesthetic by downward glances.

### Choice of idiom

I *see* . . . let's focus on . . . look into it . . . shed some light . . . ray of hope . . . light at the end of the tunnel . . .

*Sounds* good to me . . . I hear you . . . listen . . . I'd echo that . . . fine-tuning . . . not much to shout about . . . I wouldn't say that . . . let's say . . .

My *feeling* is . . . I go along with you there . . . we hit it off well . . . keep in touch . . . kick this idea around . . . can't put my finger on it . . .

NLP helps to make the vital step from 'What sort of mood is my partner in?' to 'Is there an adjustment I can make so as to harmonize more effectively with him?

## QUESTION: WHICH OF MY MANY ARGUMENTS SHOULD I MOBILIZE FOR THIS PARTNER?

One of the most widely used psychometric instruments is the Myers-Briggs inventory (MBTI), which permits the categorizing of subjects into one of 16 types, derived from four polarities. Two of the polarities permit us to divide people into four key types, particularly important when we are shaping our arguments in order to convince them. With apologies to Myers-Briggs' practitioners for a dramatic over-simplification, we offer you the opportunity to categorize yourself on this grid.

Plot yourself along the vertical – how do you make your decisions?

Factual/Steady . . . Intuitive/Impatient

and along the horizontal – what sort of information do you like to deal in?

Expert/Logical . . . Personal/Human

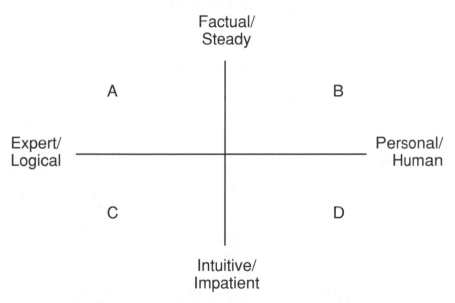

We find that this model maps very closely onto the original polarities of Edward Hall (see above). Type A personalities are the accepted norm within Low Context/ Monochronic/North-West European cultures; Type D is more at home in High Context/Polychronic/South-Eastern countries.

If you are about to meet a Swede for the first time, and wish to present a convincing case, be ready to offer:

- Up-front clarity, emphasizing specific benefits.
- Logical, checkable, achievable proposals.

- Defined project goals and agreed success measurements.

If your new partner is a Gulf Arab, and you want to tailor your arguments to suit, then concentrate on:

- The big picture and the personal touch.

- Broad recommendations, with space for your partner to fill in the details.

- Long-term qualitative advantages with mutual trust to bind the deal.

The big mistake in any act of persuasion is to pretend that your inter-locutor is the same sort of person as you. (How easy life would be! And how dull!) If you are an A type working in a D culture, or vice-versa, you have your work cut out.

## APPENDIX 3A – COMMENTARY ON 'PROVERBS' QUESTIONNAIRE

The graphs show average results from a handful of cultures: Japanese, Arab, French, Italian, Spanish, German, Swiss and British. The sample sizes were in the dozens, the respondents were all middle and senior managers involved in international business.

Individual responses can never be predicted, but some significant patterns emerge within each culture.

*TIME IS MONEY*

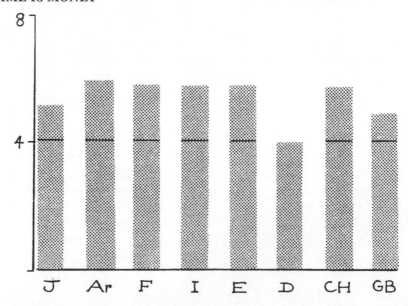

Our panel members often found themselves splitting their business view of time from their private view. Some of the scores represent an arithmetical compromise between the two.

Non-German readers might have expected Germans to endorse the time-is-money principle. A generation ago that might have been the case. Nowadays, the view tends to be: Time at work should be carefully managed in order to maximize free time. (See Chapter 5, p 101.)

## *BLOOD IS THICKER THAN WATER*

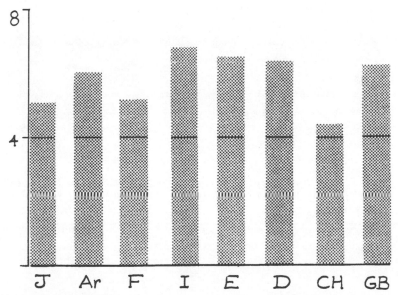

Discussion of this proverb centres on whether the family should suffer in the interests of career and company, and also on the question of nepotism.

The Arab response is perhaps surprising: the Arab way of life puts great emphasis on family, and Arab businesses are often run on family lines. But our Arab respondents are not traditional Arab merchants; they are executives working for multinational companies (mainly in Egypt and other Eastern Mediterranean countries).

## *MY WORD IS MY BOND*

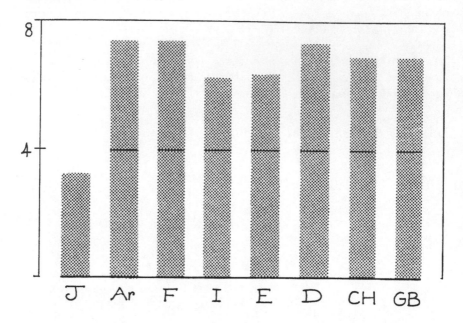

Almost all respondents value their personal reputation under this heading. Where they give a score of less than 8, they refer to the need to temper the ideal with realism.

The Japanese reaction should be seen in relation to their pragmatic, exploratory approach and to their feeling for the group. What is truth, if it disturbs the harmony?

## GOD WILL PROVIDE

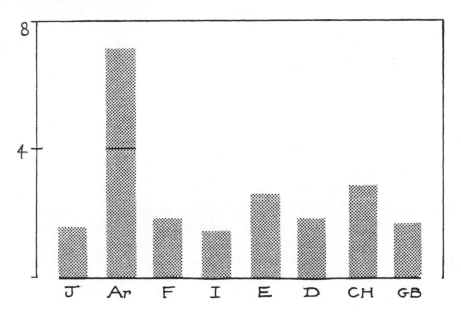

Most respondents took this in a religious sense, referring to a personal deity. Some understood it as a more general reference to the degree of push required to achieve things in life.

On this point, the Arab panel (which includes some Christians), gives a response which accords with most outsiders' expectations. Japan, in spite of frequent images in the western media of temples and meditating monks, is a highly secular society.

**DO AS YOU WOULD BE DONE BY**

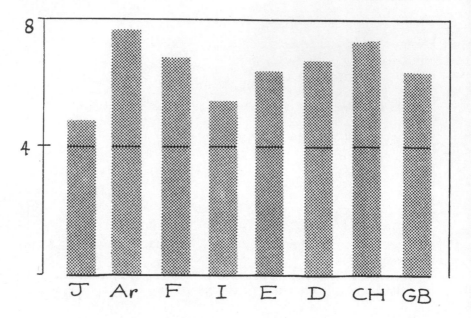

This proverb is close to the New Testament sentiment 'Love thy neighbour'. Most discussions were about fair play, and whether it helped the fair player in the long run. Some respondents, including a surprising number of native English speakers, misread the grammar of the sentence and take it to mean 'Do as you have been done by', closer to the Old Testament principle of 'An eye for an eye'. This introduces some distortion into the results. The Arabs saw it as the same as their proverb: 'treat people as you would like to be treated'.

### TRUTH IS RELATIVE

When I was studying for a Masters degree in the UK, 1 decided to carry out field research on the construction industry in Abu Dhabi. I contacted my father to help me compile a database of engineers, architects, consultants and clients. Within two weeks, my father produced a list of about 200 people. A month later, I traveled to Abu Dhabi, and with the help of my father's office, I posted my questionnaires within two days of arriving. A week went by, and I did not receive a single response. I began to contact people on my database, and the following is a typical scenario:

- Hello, may I speak to Engineer Saalim Assaf
- Speaking
- My name is Jehad Al-Omari, and I am phoning you regarding . . .
- Are you by any chance Ahmed's son?
- Yes, I am. What I wanted to talk to you about is . . .
- How is your father? I have not seen him for some time.
- He is well, and he sends his regards.
- Thank you. Please send him my regards too.
- I will. Did you receive the questionnaire that I sent you a week ago?
- What questionnaire?
- It had a covering letter from Brunel University!
- Yes, yes, I remember. I am afraid that I threw it away.
- Oh!
- I did not know it was from you. You should have phoned first.
- I am sorry. Can I send you another one?
- Yes of course. I will be waiting for it.

Two days later, Engineer Saalim Assaf telephoned me back. Here is another typical conversation:

- Hello Jehad, this is Engineer Saalim Assaf with you.
- Hello, how are you? I hope that you have now received my questionnaire.
- Yes. I have it in front of me.
- Great, no problems I hope.
- Not at all. It looks good. Why don't you come to my office to discuss it?
- This is very kind of you, but maybe another time.

- Are you sure?
- Honestly, I wish I could, but I have 200 other questionnaires that I need to chase, and I only have another week to go before I go back to London.
- OK. How do you want me to fill the questionnaire?
- Well, I would be grateful if you could give me as much detail as possible.
- Yes, yes. But what are you looking for?
- Please, can you just answer the questions as honestly and truthfully?
- But you want to pass, don't you?
- Yes I do, but it won't matter how you answer the questions!
- Are you sure?
- Yes, thank you very much.
- No problem. Please say hello to your father.
- I will.

Dr Jehad Al-Omari, Canning Combat.

# 4

# Tactics

When your preparation is complete, the great thing is to be ready to adapt your methods to the local terrain. Flexible responses are part and parcel of good tactics.

In military terms, tactical warfare brings into play three variables: strength, position and the element of surprise. If politicians make policy, and the general staff are responsible for strategy, the line officers in the field live in the sphere of Tactics. (It is the common soldiers' job to shoot straight, and the sergeants' job to keep them at it.)

If you ask three businesspeople to tell you how policy, strategy and Tactics interrelate, you will get six different answers. 'Tactics', particularly, changes according to the context in which you find it – it is a chameleon word.

The travelling businessperson at whom we have aimed this chapter is somewhere between second lieutenant and colonel. His span of control is tactical: he is mandated to make decisions of limited scope in 'real time' – reacting to changing circumstances without reference back to HQ.

We hope it will become clear that we do not equate 'real time' with 'short term'. One of the underlying messages in this chapter is this: every tactical decision made on the spot should contribute to longer-term, strategic objectives. If a field officer engages and defeats an enemy patrol, but sparks off a major battle that his own side is not prepared for, he can't expect any medals.

The other message of this chapter is: understanding and respecting your business partner's needs does not mean weakness or sentimentality. It means good business.

## LEARNING HOW

> During the negotiations we explored various avenues, and finally came up with a solution which seemed mutually beneficial.

> I took the sucker for a fortune, and the beautiful thing is he still doesn't know what happened.
>
> > Two descriptions of the same event, delivered
> > by the parties from opposite sides of the
> > negotiating table.

The first half of this book has been largely devoted to exploring the background to communication. When you have done your homework on your potential partner's background *culture*, acquainted yourself with the *company* or departmental context he comes from, and paid due consideration to his *character* (our three constant factors), you are ready to start considering your *tactics* (the first of our transient factors). Up to this point, it makes little difference whether you are preparing for a stand-up presentation, a working lunch, or a crucial round of golf.

We find that it is specifically the use of the word 'negotiation' in the title of a book or seminar which raises expectations in the area of 'tactics'. The reader or participant wants to become more competent tactically, by learning frameworks and ground-rules to give shape to his own general experience and common sense. People are given to saying 'I'm something of an amateur psychologist' without ever having read a book on the subject; similarly, they like to think of themselves as quite smart tacticians who need a little professional coaching.

Books available on negotiation are legion, and they set the tone for the seminars. There is no doubt that the clients for both are motivated by self-interest in one form or another: nobody has yet produced a business best-seller entitled *How To Be More Generous* or *How To Give The Other Chap More and Take Less Yourself*. Conversely, we have yet to come across a course in 'How to cheat, lie and retire early', or 'How to trample the other guy under foot'. The promotional leaflets tend to feature handshakes rather than clenched fists, and the 'win:win' approach is usually favoured: if we can find a way to enlarge the pie, we can both get a bigger piece.

This 'green negotiator' ideal fits the spirit of the times, and the management training courses we run in many countries confirm that the vintage travels well. The participants, from anywhere in the world, quickly learn that 'give and take' is different from 'push and pull', and that nice guys need not be losers.

## A 'PURE' NEGOTIATION

This is an exercise of classic simplicity, used by game theorists and negotiations analysts to explore questions of trust/suspicion, appeasement/aggression and forgiveness/punishment.

Two players, A and B, are each offered the choice of bidding X or Y. Both are aware of the scoring system:

| A bids | B bids | A scores | B scores |
| --- | --- | --- | --- |
| X | X | 3 | 3 |
| X | Y | 1 | 4 |
| Y | X | 4 | 1 |
| Y | Y | 2 | 2 |

Bids are simultaneous, and the score is reckoned up after each round.

(If you want to run it yourself, have A and B sit back to back, each equipped with a pair of flash-cards – X and Y, or Red and Blue. Each player holds one card aloft on the command 'Bid!' from the referee. The score-board should be visible to both.)

In a typical game of 10 rounds, then, there are 60 points potentially available for distribution – both players bidding X throughout, and scoring $10 \times 3$ each. Of course, this produces neither 'winner' nor 'loser', but a high score for both players.

This 'perfect score' rarely happens. Players are slow to see the $X + X = $ *benefits for all* equation, and often even slower to implement it, since bidding X entails a risk – not only of forsaking one point, but also of permitting the 'enemy' to develop a three-point lead.

A comparative analysis (Carlisle and Parker, *Beyond Negotiation*) focused on precisely this: how early in the game, if ever, will a player bid X? The comparison, made over several thousand runs of the game, was between British and American players.

Before you read the next paragraph, close your eyes and think: which of the two cultures is more likely to play in the spirit of 'I win – you lose' (ie avoid X bids)?

In the first round, 27 per cent of American players bid X, as against only 15 per cent British. Within the first four rounds, 80 per cent of Americans took the risk at least once, as against only 40 per cent of British.

So, did you guess right? What stereotype or model were you drawing on?

'Uncertainty tends to produce conservative behaviour', observes Carlisle, and goes on to speculate about the British class system leading to ingrained mutual suspicion between employers and unions, and thence between customers and suppliers. If that hypothesis is not sufficient to explain this apparently destructive pattern of behaviour among British players: 'There is another conjecture: that the British do not really wish to take responsibility for a long-term relationship which is of relative equality. They actually prefer the arm's length relationship, not because it is, on the face of it, more cost effective, but because they cannot risk "getting involved" . . . It is safer to "play games" '.

By this interpretation, the *playing the game* idea which is traditionally associated with the British is not necessarily a creative way of securing the best deal for everybody.

It is worth noting that the evidence for these conclusions was a set of results from within each culture – British negotiating with British, Americans with Americans. Our own observations have usually been of negotiations between cultures. The transactions we have observed usually involve more complicated factors than the game described here.

The exercise, known as 'The Prisoners' Dilemma', is rich in source material for the behavioural scientist. Dissertations have been written, television programmes produced, and computer models developed. Computer simulation reveals that the most successful strategy long-term is tit-for-tat: open with an X (offering to be a Nice Guy) and then mirror the other player's bids (avoiding becoming a Victim). It opens the way to healthy scoring and and protects you from too heavy a beating by Y bids.

Meanwhile, in those rounds where you meet another Nice Guy, you can profit from each other's co-operative approaches.

So in the long term, the Nice Guys as a group tend to rise to the top, leaving the others behind in a welter of mistrust.

## KNOW YOUR OWN ATTITUDE

> You must become a new kind of Scandinavian. You must develop the killer instinct. You must learn to love manipulating people.
> Human Resource Director in a major Swedish company,
> addressing the latest intake of university graduates

Comments like these provide clues to a person's view of business: 'He's a great engineer, but he's too honest to make a good salesman'; 'I'm worried about your attitude – you seem to be determined to tell the client the truth, even when he hasn't asked for it'; 'It's one big game, so don't get all tangled up in ethics'; 'Tell them what they want to hear, that's the trick'; 'It's dog eat dog out there'.

Where do you draw the line between persuasion and manipulation? Between manipulation and cheating? Unless you have a fairly clear view of your own values, limitations and sticking points, you are a danger to yourself in negotiations.

Of course, if you *are* out for a quick killing, you must have that clear in your mind from the outset. Uncertainty guarantees failure.

Yet being nice, building a reputation for honesty, is not simple dumb altruism. Typically, a mature business gets 80 per cent of its orders from established clients, and this puts a premium on good long-term relationships.

## KNOW YOUR PARTNER'S ATTITUDE

Outside the training centre and the seminar suite, we hear stories of shady dealing from the people we meet along the way ('You train people in negotiations, do you? Here's one for you: a friend of mine . . . well, a friend of a friend, actually, but anyway . . .').

We have been involved in conversations, particularly in the airport bar at Helsinki, where the Nordic sauna has been discussed. There is a commonly held view that an invitation to the sauna has a more sinister purpose than simple hygiene and relaxation. 'It's a way of breaking down your resistance, you see. They're used to seeing each other with nothing on, so they know they're at an advantage – a territorial thing. Anyway, how can you maintain your dignity in the next day's negotiations if you think they've been comparing notes about your anatomy?'

Similarly with the Russians and alcohol. 'That banquet on the last day! Eight glasses lined up beside each plate, for different types of vodka. We'd been warned, of course. All designed to get you paralytic and then catch you off your guard. It's water being poured into the other side's glasses.'

The sauna is an important social focus in Finland. Formal hospitality in Russia demands lots of toasts. Those who claim to have detected ulterior motives are actually telling us quite a lot about their own hang-ups.

There are, of course, massive local variations in what is ethical or respectable in business; different cultures have different thresholds for trickery, confrontation and gamesmanship.

### UNEVEN PLAYING FIELDS

> Sure, I've got a lot of time for the 'win:win' school. Only trouble is,
> when one of these kids comes up against an 'I win:you lose' merchant
> – some caveman who can't even *spell* Harvard – then you get zero
> communication. They're playing different games.
>
> Senior executive, Port of New York Authority

The British comedian, Peter Sellers, was immensely popular in Sweden,
but one of his classic films was never released there: *I'm All Right, Jack*, in
which he portrays Fred Kite, union shop steward in England's dark days
of class war and demarcation dispute. We ran the film once for a group
of Stockholm businesspeople, to gauge their reaction: which was per-
plexity and horror in equal amounts. Not funny at all. This was socially
insane behaviour: non-productive conflict.

After the turmoil in France in 1968, the government promised many
reforms, including a loosening of its grip over television, which many
radicals saw as a propaganda tool for whichever party was in power. They
looked across the Channel to study the apparently much healthier situation in the UK. To their consternation, they found that the British government had even greater powers over the BBC according to the BBC's
charter than had the French government over ORTF. The point was that
no British government had ever used those powers to the full. The
observers concluded that such a system (or lack of system) could not work
in France. The French use a franglais word – *le fairplay* – to describe the
British arrangement.

(If this example of harmony and understanding in British institutions
seems to contradict the Peter Sellers example which precedes it, consider
the class system and its effects: the government in Whitehall and the
BBC's upper echelons were predominantly staffed – some would say they
still are – by members of a class élite. 'Fair play' meant little in the world
of Fred Kite – or if it did, it did not apply to his dealings with those from
outside his own class.)

Outsiders can fare badly in negotiations with East Asian cultures which
are rooted in Confucianism. The system has, at its heart, strict ideas of fil-
ial piety and duty both upwards and downwards. The vertical bonds that
run father-to-son-to-grandson are exclusive; no matter how you handle
yourself during business dealings, you cannot become your trading partner's son or father. There is no code of conduct for 'proper' dealings with
outsiders, and so xenophobia has a free rein. In Japan there is a saying:
*Hito-wo mitara doroboro omoe* (Treat a stranger like a thief.)

The *gwailoh* (long-nosed devil) negotiating with the Chinese sometimes
experiences rough treatment. It is said that a recent Hong Kong gover-
nor suffered a heart attack in Beijing during negotiations over 1997. The
Chinese delegation listened to his side's point of view in silence for a

while, and then suddenly exploded in an unstoppable torrent of vitu-
peration. This style of negotiation is not 'win:win', it is 'I win: you can take
care of yourself if you like.'

Japan was closed to foreigners for 265 years up to 1868. During that
time, the Japanese learned strict control of their facial expressions and
body language, enabling them in the last 120 years to suppress any dis-
taste they feel at dealing with *gaijin* (foreigners). This is just as well, for
where China is self-sufficient in all raw materials, Japan has a transfor-
mation economy, so its representatives must always be prepared to seek
out the best deal with foreign suppliers or customers. If this attitude leads
to a 'win:win' contract, then well and good – but it will be for reasons of
pragmatism, rather than from any desire to 'do the right thing' by the
stranger.

The refined principle of group decison-making so typical of Japan's
overcrowded island carries the label *wa* (harmony). It expresses itself
most obviously in quiet speech, modest conduct, and refined good manners. We have worked with many Japanese preparing for long postings
to Europe or the US, and know well the difficulty they have in saying 'No'
to a business partner's face. This inhibition is not present in the Chinese.

## KNOW YOUR PARTNER'S BARGAINING RANGE

In mature markets, we might expect our negotiating partner to move just
a bit on price factors, but that doesn't apply everywhere.

> Let me tell you the difference. American negotiation: the first Amer-
> ican says 10 and the second American says No. So the first comes
> down to 9.95. Russian negotiation: the first Russian says 10 and the
> second Russian says No. So the first comes down to 5. The Russians
> are fumbling; they don't really know the value of what they're trad-
> ing. There's no market price to take as a benchmark . . .
>
> Russian manager in Ekaterinburg

If you go into a negotiation prepared for tiny marginal movements, while
your customer is sharpening a big knife, there is little hope of a happy
outcome. In such situations there is no substitute for a local fixer – but
you must be prepared to listen to what he says.

> It happened with a Scandinavian company we were consulting for –
> a heavy engineering group, hungry for business in Asia. They
> retained a Singapore Chinese salesman, who had a hot prospect.
> Naturally he wanted a rough price to go in with, and experience told
> him to expect a 20 per cent reduction in the course of the negotia-
> tion. No, no, said head office: get a precise specification from the
> client, then we will calculate a realistic price. Our experience shows
> that a 5 per cent movement is a kind of ethical limit. Otherwise it's

dirty tricks, isn't it? If we name too high a price, we look greedy. If it's too low, the customer will have us over a barrel. More information, before we move. The customer got fed up and bought from Korea. We were called in to figure out what went wrong. All the Scandinavians found the 5 per cent figure to be fair and realistic. All the British, Dutch and Italians saw things the Chinese way: 20 per cent is just part of the ritual.

Gerard Bannon, Canning consultant

# DELIVER YOUR MESSAGE TO SUIT YOUR PARTNER

It is difficult to get people to understand *abstract, unfamiliar* ideas. All kinds of teachers have faced this problem, and come up with the same answer: you have to translate your *abstract unfamiliar* proposition into terms which are *concrete* and *familiar* to your student.

Travelling salesmen carry cases of samples and photographic pamphlets. Their tubes of toothpaste or their toothpaste-making machines are *concrete* enough, but they are *unfamiliar* to the customer. He won't buy until he has seen them at least, and preferably touched them, so that they become *familiar*. Then he can understand and remember the commercial benefits.

The vicar's sermon is usually on a standard theological theme – an *abstract* idea, which will be quite *familiar* to his congregation. It is his job to bring the idea to life and help his flock absorb the spiritual benefits. To do so he must express the *abstract* in terms of the *concrete*. He relies on symbols – the Lamb, the Cross, the Trinity – and he tells simple stories about fishermen, soldiers, rich men, poor men, prodigal sons and loyal daughters.

The American management consultant working in the post-communist world (or the Jesuit missionary up the Orinoco) has a double problem to solve: his ideas are both *abstract* and *unfamiliar*. He sometimes makes the mistake of offering concrete examples from an unfamiliar world, which only confuses the client further: what can an Albanian make of a metaphor based on a California lifestyle (or what can a jungle Indian make of the parable of the talents)?

The only route from *abstract/unfamiliar* to the zone of real communication lies through the *abstract/familiar* quadrant. To explain the unfamiliar abstract of *acceleration*, the physics teacher combines two abstracts which the pupils are already comfortable with: *speed* and *time*. Then it is time to talk about dropping cannonballs from the Leaning Tower, and the performance of drag racers. There is no point in describing the actions of particles and waves which the pupils have never encountered before.

Back in the 70s, I was working as a teaching volunteer in a big village on the edge of the Kalahari – about 40,000 people. The US Peace

Corp sent in a fresh team, including Jim – a bright, enthusiastic maths teacher – or 'math' as they say. After two weeks he was dispirited: 'Hey, I know I shouldn't say it, but are these kids stupid? I mean they understand nothing.' We were up in the hills above the village, and we sat for a while looking at the view. Suddenly Jim leapt to his feet and cursed his own stupidity. He ran all the way back to the school, and I didn't see him again until the next morning, grinning triumphantly after his first class.

It was the geometry that was the real problem. Botswana had only been independent for a few years and was still using the curriculum of its British colonial masters: geometry based on a Greek model. Think of Greek architecture; think of the layout of an English new town. For Jim's pupils, the concept of a right angle had no real meaning. So on that Monday morning, Jim asked them to imagine they were an eagle flying over the village, and to draw what they would see. They drew circles, of course, and he began to teach them about *pi*. Later they learned about radii, diameters and tangents before moving on to right angles and squares.

Richard Pooley, Canning consultant

## Where Real Communication Happens

| | Familiar | Unfamiliar |
|---|---|---|
| **Concrete** | **Simple Sketches** ← **Stories About Real People** ↑ ↖ | *Travelling Salesman* Photographs Samples Commercial Benefits |
| **Abstract** | *Vicar in his Church* Parables Symbols Spiritual Benefits | *Consultant in Tomsk* Abstract ideas from an Unfamiliar World No Communication Go to Concrete Ideas, Familiar Territory |

The best, most subtle tactics are based on an understanding of the other party's motivations, taking into account factors of background culture, business context, and individual character.

*The Man Who Never Was*, the true story of a counter-intelligence plot, includes the following paragraphs concerning a plan to confuse the enemy with a misleading document:

> You are a British Intelligence Officer; you have an opposite number in the enemy Intelligence, say (as in the last war), in Berlin; and above him is the German Operational command. What you, a Briton with a British background, think can be deduced from a document does not matter. It is what *your opposite number*, with his German knowledge and background, will think that matters – what construction he will put on the document. Therefore, if you want him to think such-and-such a thing, you must give him something which will make him (and not you) think it.
>
> But he may be suspicious and want confirmation; you must think out what enquiries will be made (not what enquiries would you make) and give him the answers to those enquiries so as to satisfy him. In other words, you must remember that a German does not think and react as an Englishman does, and you must put yourself into his mind.

## CASE STUDY

The Danish salesman knew his machine well, and he knew it could turn out 10,000 egg-boxes an hour working at full capacity.

The Soviet factory manager liked the machine, knew its capacity, and had insisted on an extension of the guarantee period: any running faults in the first three years, and a Danish engineer would be flown out to fix it – at the expense of the supplier.

'So, all is agreed, then. My congratulations. Now, if you can stand it, I would like to invite you to one further meeting tomorrow. Concerning the maximum productive capacity.'

'Of course, but I thought everything was clear.'

'Between you and me, yes. But there will be another person at the meeting tomorrow – a representative from the regional collective. When I ask you how many units per hour the machine will turn out, I suggest you adjust your answer.'

'Above 10,000, I'm afraid, things will start to go wrong.'

'You see, this representative will set my production targets next year. And higher targets the year after. If we *start* at 10,000, we can be sure of breakdowns very soon – meaning production hold-ups for me, and great expense for you under the terms of the guarantee.'

'I see. How would 8,000 sound?'

'Exactly the figure I had in mind.'

The Soviet was buying more than an egg-box machine. He was buying a couple of years free of stress in the centrally planned economy.

# LIVE FOR THE DAY AFTER TOMORROW

Tactics are mainly to do with action in the short term. But the skilful tactician keeps a clear eye on the long-term effects.

Good tactics may even include the sacrifice of some small immediate gain in the name of a long-term relationship.

### CASE STUDY

It's 2 am. A British salesman and his Spanish client stroll through the cobbled alleyways of ancient Toledo, their conversation ranging from the marvels of the city's architecture, to the impact of 1992 on the Spanish economy, to the personal foibles of business acquaintances – including the Spaniard's CEO, who is to put in an appearance at tomorrow's meeting.

Not a natural nightbird, the Brit is apprehensive. Is he being softened up before the crucial stages of the negotiation? It was certainly a good dinner . . .

Next day, the CEO cuts the proposal to ribbons beneath the pitying gaze of the salesman's host, who escorts the victim to the airport. 'Don't worry. All that's needed is a price-cut, so Mr Big can feel his intervention was effective . . .'

Sure enough, after a cosmetic adjustment in the terms, the deal is agreed by fax and phone within a week – delivery immediate, payment on the nail.

---

The faint odour of plastic warmed by halogen lighting. The office of a West German middle manager, who throws a barrage of objections at the British offer: 'How can this possibly work? . . . incompatible with procedures . . . this is too extensive . . . that is insufficient . . . this we already have . . . that we do not need . . .'

The wipe-clean day planner on the wall allocates 45 minutes, and the salesman is duly shown out, clutching an armful of technical brochures as consolation. Correspondence continues for 18 months before any German commitment is made.

The salesman's worries during that time include: Why did they seem to understand so little about our service? What do they really think of our price? Why are they taking so long to decide?

Both Spanish and German deals resulted from successful negotiations. Similar product, same salesman. Two rather different countries, just one day's drive apart.

The variations between the two experiences fall into four categories:

- relationship

- hierarchy

- timing

- price/specification.

The *relationship* in the Spanish case was based on a strong degree of personal intimacy before any real business started. The local style is first to develop trust – chatting, sharing little secrets, spending hours over meals together – before the pocket calculators come out. Even then, every opportunity is taken to make the personal bond even tighter between the two people, as opposed to the two organizations.

In the German case, there was a cup of coffee as commercial discussions began. Much later, when business (and repeat business) was being done, the Brit was invited for chummy evenings in German homes – a form of business hospitality much more common there than in Spain.

A *hierarchy* was manifest in the Spanish set-up: the big boss came to show his authority (and size the salesman up). The CEO never appeared again after the first chilly meeting. He had served his purpose as the mouthpiece of the company. In the German case, authority had been delegated in a neat package: Investigate this supplier; if OK, report back; if not OK, look for others. The real decision maker was beyond the salesman's reach, and only broke cover at a later stage in the dealings.

*Timing* worked very differently in the two countries. In Toledo, there was a full day of discussion (on top of the previous evening's entertainment), during which the agenda suggested by the British salesman was warmly received, then largely ignored. Quick results thereafter. In Cologne, the 45-minute meeting adhered to the agreed timetable point by point, but left a great deal of exploration still to be done before a deal could be struck. (Much more about timing in Chapter 5.)

The German negotiator paid great attention to the *specification*, seeking weak points, and making it clear that his company would impose their requirements in certain areas before any deal was remotely possible. Fairly late in the proceedings, he asked for a *price*, remarked that it was in the higher range of his expectations, and made no attempt to bring it down.

His Spanish counterparts seemed to assume that their would-be suppliers knew their job, and were content to leave the detailed specifications to them. The pressure was all on price. The British company came close to losing the deal because they had made a firm price statement rather early and left themselves short of manoeuvring space.

# 5

# Timing

In global dealings, time is the most noticeable aspect of distance. As you travel, take into account the shifting attitudes to time. When you arrive, make your arrangements about time to fit the local mood.

The clock, not the steam engine, is the key machine of the modern industrial age.

L. Mumford

Potatoes, enclosed in a black box, still respond chemically to the changes of night and day outside. Oysters, removed from their natural waters to a distant laboratory, maintain their feeding rhythms to match favourable tidal times 'back home'. Jet-lag is a problem for some international executives. All living things have an internal clock.

Man has taken his practical measurements of passing time from nature: the solar year, the lunar month (or some calendar compromise), night and day. The hour, the minute and the second were conceived of in

97

Ancient Babylon, but they couldn't measure them. Roman hours varied in length with the season: there were always 12 hours to the night.

Until the 18th century, the time of day was largely a local concern. The village clock was set in accordance with its longitudinal position – which dictated the rising and the setting of the sun as the Earth spun on its axis – and if all agreed that the village clock was correct, that was good enough. The mail-coach system, moving fast enough to cause a problem with time, solved the problem by issuing the coachman with a clock that could be set to gain or lose as he travelled between villages. De Quincey wrote of 'the conscious presence of a central intellect that in the midst of vast distance, of storms, of darkness, of danger – overruled all obstacles into one steady co-operation to a national result.'

The clockmakers were also encouraged for supranational reasons. The Spanish and the English monarchs offered prizes for ever more accurate chronometers – not to work out what time it was at a fixed point on the globe, but rather the reverse: being sure what time it was, navigators could be more sure of where they were. A crossing to Jamaica in 1762 shipped a chronometer accurate to within five seconds.

A century later, 'local time' and 'railroad time' operated side by side in the US – often with more than one railroad time in operation at busy interchanges like Pittsburgh. Time zone formalities were adopted in the US in 1883. A year later, the world accepted Greenwich Mean Time as a global reference point – partly in recognition of British flair in chronometry. That flair was closely linked with the Royal Navy's mastery of the sea.

Not all the world accepted GMT unhesitatingly, however. Germany only abolished its five internal time zones in 1891, and France resisted cross-Channel time until 1911.

> By a pardonable reticence, the law abstained from saying that the time so defined is that of Greenwich, and our self-respect can pretend that we have adopted the time of Argentan.
> L. Houllevique, in *La Revue de Paris*, 1913

Since then the story has been one of increasing standardization and simplification. For philosophers and mathematicians, or in the rarefied atmosphere of physics, time might remain a complex puzzle to be solved, but for everyday practical purposes man has got time licked.

Yet time – and the way it is handled – is still a troublesome area of friction between individuals and cultures.

> I've been living in Germany now for almost 20 years, and have settled in well – yet I'm still annoyed at how parochial the national television is: so little information about the world outside, although the whole country is full of immigrants like me. Last week, for example, they gave about 30 seconds at the end of the news to developments in the Middle East, and then devoted a whole sixty-minute

programme to the Millennium Bug – what a disaster it might be for German industry, the German economy, German society. It's only a question of computer software – electrons in a machine. And thousands of specialists have been fixing it for years now. How can anybody really care about such a thing?

Iranian manager in multinational company

---

### TIME AND COURTSHIP

Social observers in the early 1940s found a strange mixture of attitudes among young people in the South West of England. Almost all the young men were American – servicemen based there during the build-up to the Normandy invasion. The young women were either local girls, or teenagers evacuated from the vulnerable cities.

Small-town America, at that period, was not notable for a climate of sexual freedom or loose living, yet the boys soon earned a reputation for being 'fast'. The English girls they were dating, meanwhile, were described back on the base as 'easy', although the girls' families were certainly quite respectable, and there was a clear distinction between 'a nice girl' and a tramp.

The observers investigated.

They found that there were approximately 30 stages of courtship, in both cultures, from first eye contact to full sexual intercourse. However, kissing came much earlier – was more 'innocent' – in the American than in the English arrangement (say step 5 as opposed to 25).

So there was confusion over 'how far do you go and how fast?' The American boy, claiming a kiss on the first date, did not feel he was pushing his luck. The English girl had to choose: slap his face, or offer more than either he or she had originally intended. Probably the slapped faces were not reported back at camp.

Differing attitudes to time lead to a great deal of unnecessary distress.

# SET YOUR WATCH TO LOCAL TIME

I used to go to Yugoslavia quite a lot. It would take me about three days each trip to slow down to the Balkan pace of life, and I felt really ratty until I'd made the adjustment. Eventually, I trained myself consciously to adjust my body clock, tranquillizing myself as the JAT pilots scraped over the Alpine summits with inches to spare.

Bill Reed, Canning consultant

The case study in Chapter 4 – that of the salesman in Germany and Spain – touched on the central issue here: what comes first, business or people? The answer is never straightforward, as the two considerations are so closely intertwined.

The Westerner on a business secondment in *Japan* goes through stages: 'It's the same for everybody. Six days here and you're terribly confused. Another six months and you're ready to write a book explaining it all. Six years after that you're terribly confused . . .'

Look beneath the superficial frenzy of life in the big Japanese cities, and you find long working days (12 hours is typical) and long careers (a lifetime in the same company). They use the time to build harmonious agreements upon harmonious relationships.

Which means, effectively, putting people first. Somewhere between the apparently inconclusive meetings and the final business decision, the Western visitor may feel he is wasting yet more time on dinners and drinking sessions during the hours of *breiko* after the official working day is over. But that time is far from wasted. The rather stiff conventions of office life fall away, and the people can get in touch with each other.

If the business proposal under consideration now means working together in the future the Japanese feel that no decision can be taken until the people involved know each other. This does not mean that the entertainments in the geisha house or karaoke bar are a specific test. It simply makes sense to have these bonding experiences as part of the development of a good working relationship.

> It takes time to build, but it's powerful once it's in place. I recently had the opportunity to do a deal in Japan without consulting my partner there. Not with his direct competitors or anything, just a piece of business in the same market. I had to offer it to him first, although it wasn't really his sort of deal. He would have been horrified if the first he'd known was seeing the goods in the store. We've taken years to build this trust, and you don't just throw it away.
>
> Italian manufacturer of kitchen equipment

The *German* approach to time is highly structured with careful scheduling. Delegation, although practised with thoroughness, usually has strings attached. This can make innovative decisions painful, as the subordinate's decision time with his boss is kept separate from his communication time with you. The junior has full authority over an agreed range of decisions, but that range can never include the unexpected. If he takes the conservative path, and blocks the upward progress of your surprise proposal ('I am not empowered to bring this matter to my boss's attention'), you are stuck. Even if you try the back door, and the boss likes the idea, he will be reluctant to overrule his subordinate. The economic emergency of the post-war years, when rules were frequently broken in order to get an urgent job done, was a long time ago.

The German attitude to time is changing. They leave the office on time and award themselves generous holidays.

> Japanese competition is really unfair. We work efficiently; they work efficiently *and long*.
>
> Senior manager, German car firm

---

**INTERCULTURAL TIME STRESS**

*AN EXERCISE*

You are in charge of a multinational team – based in France – who are designing and implementing a new IT system for a Korean client. The system is to coordinate the distribution of electronic consumer goods throughout the European market.

The team has been together for six weeks now and already there are signs of serious friction. At a client meeting two days ago, references were made to a *lack of communication* within your team. Your main Korean client, over dinner later, was much more blunt: *Sometimes we are asked the same question by two or three different people. Our time is being wasted. It needs to be better coordinated. One of your people is always blaming the others when there are problems. This is not good teamwork.*

The person Mr Kim was referring to is Klaus Alexander. He is a Developer/Analyst – technically one of the best. He came to you after doing an excellent job on a similar project for a Finnish client in Helsinki. Now, though, he appears to have difficulty accepting the rather different attitudes to work processes displayed by members of the team. He sticks rigidly to schedules, sneers at anybody who arrives late at the office or for meetings, and has no patience with anyone who fails to meet his own self-imposed deadlines. He insists on his right to go home no later than 1700, even if it means leaving some vital work half-finished.

> When you have tackled him about this in the past, he has said he cannot be made to work late because of the inefficiency of others. He is a crucial member of your team, but his behaviour is lowering morale and disrupting the whole project.
>
> How can you persuade him to be more flexible in his approach and more appreciative of the way other people do things?

Speed in decision-making is in inverse proportion to bureaucracy. *North American* industry is often hung on top-down decision-making systems; 'why change a winning formula?' is a rhetorical question most frequently asked by the man at the top who invented the formula. For all their protestations about time being money, American middle managers frequently disappoint by their hesitations and procrastination.

> About the only thing that really does move faster in US industry is the revolving door marked In and Out. There's really no stigma attached when the company lets you go . . . some ways it has a kind of cachet about it: 'I was a real risk-taker, see, and I took one risk too many.'
>
> American manager,
> currently running ice-cream plant in New Jersey

Steady *Sweden*, on the other hand, where you never see anybody running along a corporate corridor, scores well on power devolution. The social systems are based on consensus, and this is reflected in a general absence of fear in the ranks of the big companies.

> I give the matter due thought, and then, within reasonable limits, agree to what seems right to me. There are very few sanctions against me if I make a mistake – who ever gets sacked in Sweden?
>
> Training manager, light engineering firm, Malmö

We have heard Swedes at international conventions criticize their American colleagues for moving too slowly. It must be said, however, that carrots are also in short supply in Sweden, just as sticks are. There is little inducement to move particularly fast.

*Spain* has dramatically changed gear. Business there is in a hurry. Apart from less industrialized areas like Andalusia and Galicia, the stereotypical *mañana* image is completely, probably irreversibly, out of date.

Yet the traditions of hospitality, and pleasure in unhurried conversation, persist. The commonest error among business visitors to Spain is to interpret this as a symptom of a lackadaisical attitude overall. Beware.

Once the essentials (taking care of people, primarily) have been dealt with, decisions are swift and action energetic.

Energy and decisiveness characterized the *British* in Queen Victoria's day. Amiability and procrastination are their hallmarks nowadays. *Holland* and Britain are near neighbours, both geographically and culturally:

> We have no difficulty getting on with our British colleagues, they're much the same as us – except they do go on about weather and the motorways for ages before getting down to business.
>
> Dutch engineer in petroleum company

Timing in the Arab world often trips up the inexperienced negotiator from elsewhere. Social, business and general matters rub against each other in apparently random order – a kind of 'circular agenda' is the best description. A point will arise, get an airing, and then vanish, only to resurface in a different form later in the discussion.

Your Arab partner operates in 'real time' more readily than, say, a North European: he has no fixed objective, but a dazzling speed in producing and processing new options during the meeting.

---

### DINNER AT ED'S

I shall never forget the first time I was invited, with another Arab friend, to a dinner in an English house. Ed, our host, sensed that we were feeling homesick and invited us to meet his family. We were very surprised that the dinner date was fixed three weeks in advance You won't catch many Arabs planning a dinner date that far in advance. The essence of hospitality is spontaneity.

Anyway, we went to great trouble to buy a bottle of wine for Ed, flowers for his wife and chocolates for his children. I may add that this is not the custom back in Jordan. In the Arab world, the guest is king, and he does not need to bring presents with him, especially wine. We were invited to arrive at seven in the evening, so we made the assumption that we would not be eating until 8.30 or 9.00. We had a snack on the way! It was common sense to us that the host would entertain us for a couple of hours before the meal, and once we had eaten our meal, we would drink our coffee and depart. After all, that is the Arab way, and we did not know better. In the Arab world timing rather than time dictates the correct moment to serve dinner. If the mood is good, the conversation is flowing and the guests are relaxed, the host may decide to delay the dinner, and thus capture the moment.

Having arrived at the appointed time, it took our hosts no more than 15 minutes to lay down the meal. Apart from being totally stuffed, we were unsure about two things. Our host invited us to help ourselves, and kept trying to talk to us throughout the meal. In the Arab world, a good host will spend most of his time piling up his guests' plates, and will eat slowly in order to outlast the greediest of his guests!

Having finished our meal some 30 minutes later, we were ushered to the sitting room where coffee was served. By that time, I was looking forward to my first cigarette of the evening, so I took my pack out of my pocket. To my horror, our host glared at it and said, 'Sorry, but you can't smoke in my house'. I felt as if he had slapped me. I wanted to shout at him: I am your guest, how dare you insult me in your house? Needless to say the evening was a disaster and we left immediately after coffee. Despite this, we stayed friends with Ed, and I have visited him many times since.

Dr Jehad Al-Omari, Canning consultant

## TIME TRICKS

Books and courses on negotiation sometimes stress 'dirty tricks' which might be used to apply psychological pressure. As consultants in the international field, we are frequently asked to comment on such matters: is my negotiating opponent from culture x, y or z taking unfair advantage of me? Am I being manipulated in some way I don't understand?

Frequently the answer is 'No, your discomfort is not the result of a deliberate ploy. Rather, you are feeling oversensitive as a result of culture-shock, and your foreign partner is behaving perfectly normally in his own terms.' Typically, the misunderstanding involves differing attitudes to *time*.

### 1. SO SORRY TO KEEP YOU WAITING . . .

He leaves you in the hallway for what seems like a long, long time. Clearly he hopes to make you feel inferior, in preparation for bullying you.

**Response:** If you are visiting a time-stressed culture, you are probably wrong – he is simply busy, running behind schedule, and innocent of any crude psychological warfare. If you are visiting a culture with a more relaxed attitude, your suspicions are equally groundless, and you have failed to adjust your rhythms: in similar circumstances, he would be perfectly happy to wait. Either way, no response necessary.

### 2. I DON'T FEEL THIS IS THE RIGHT MOMENT . . .

He persistently refuses to address the key issue, giving no reason for his procrastination. Most likely he's playing for time . . .

**Response:** Convince yourself he isn't playing games. Quite possibly, he doesn't think that this is the right time. He doesn't know you well enough to want to launch deep into business. You are probably going too fast: slow down, pace yourself. It is also possible that he may need to refer the matter to a superior, but he is too embarrassed to admit that. In all circumstances, remember ***FACE-PACE***. Both are crucial to doing business with the Arabs and many of the Asian cultures.

### 3. I REALLY MUST TAKE YOU TO SEE THE BICYCLE FACTORY . . .

His scheme seems clear. He wants to waste time until you are about to leave, and then pile the pressure on – knowing you would hate to go home empty-handed.

**Response:** Either 'No, we really must get down to business now', or (if the deal is important enough) 'Wonderful, but before we go, could I just ring the airline to postpone my flight home?'. His 'scheme' is probably in your imagination. Those who claim to have suffered from this trick usually set the scene in China – in the days when an over-run exit visa was a real disaster.

### QUIZ: WHICH NATIONALITY IS THE OBJECT OF THESE COMMENTS?

(Answers: Appendix 5A)

1. 'No good trying to telephone them on a Friday afternoon; they're all off to the islands for the weekend.

2. 'A breakfast meeting, he suggested. Breakfast! Can you imagine!'

3. 'He seemed to think sticking to the agenda was more important than solving the problem.'

4. 'Work hard? Yes, they work hard – if by that you mean spending long hours at the office . . .'

5. 'The tea-break mentality. Drives you crazy!'

6.  'The hardest thing I've ever been asked to do: they wanted me to make an after-dinner speech at 7 pm.'

7.  'No, no. Any time but July. Forget July. Waste of time.'

8.  'In the cities, it's fine. But in the small towns in the valleys, it seems like every second day's a saint's day. No business.'

9.  'Bustle, bustle, bustle. Makes them feel important. But try to pin them down and what do you get?: "I can't decide without instructions from my boss, and he's away at a conference".'

10. 'Protestant work ethic? What does that mean nowadays? Get the job done so you can leave before the rush-hour starts.'

## PACING YOUR PRESENTATION

Clever public speakers and teachers deliver their important points early, and reiterate them at the end. They know that these are the moments when their listeners are most alert.

The attention/retention curve for a typical European and American audience (either of 1 or of 100) looks like this:

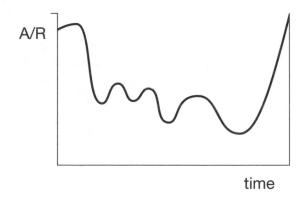

In practical terms this means that your listeners pay attention to what they are told at the beginning of a session, doze off a little after that (as every public speaker knows), and perk up again when the end is in sight.

As for retention, we meet here evidence of what psychologists call 'primacy' and 'recency'. These factors affect memory over much longer time-scales, too. When we revise for examinations at the end of a three-year course, we find the first term's work (primacy) and yesterday's input (recency) much fresher in our minds than the material we encountered a year ago.

Nobody wants the mid afternoon slot on a day-long seminar. If you are stuck with it, change something: the lighting, the layout of the chairs, your visual aids. Instructors in the armed forces know this well. It was they who first inserted nude pin-ups into their lectures to wake the lads up a bit. So one creates a series of peaks:

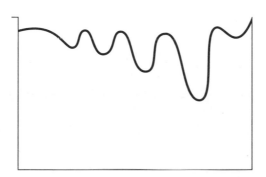

## Local variation: Japan

Our Canning colleagues in Tokyo ran tests on Japanese business executives. The resulting curve averaged out like this:

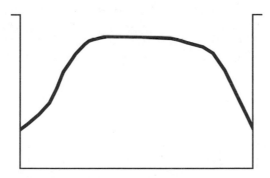

The overall pattern is virtually the reverse of what we have been seeing from Westerners.

Richard Pooley, a Canning consultant who has sat through many Japanese presentations, offered these explanations:

The first thing to mention is the stress laid on rote learning in Japanese education. They do have very good aural retention. So that might give us a flat curve: they don't draw blanks the way we do.

Now the peak in the middle – or rather the relatively poor performance at the two ends: what you get at these stages of a Japanese presentation is a lot of formalities with no real message. They like to spend the first part giving credit to everyone who has contributed – '*nemawashi*\* has happened' – and establishing their own right to be up there speaking. Everybody nods politely, but they're saving their 'active listening' for the vital middle period – the meaty bit. Once that's over, it's back to the formalities . . .

Japanese friends were amazed at the Western curve: surely intelligent people can concentrate better than that?

The idea of 'State your message, develop it, re-state it in your summary' was quite alien to them.

Now I understand why my British colleagues become agitated when listening to Japanese speakers . . .

Head of sales,
Tokyo office of UK pharma company

# AGENDA

### *AGENDA ITEM ONE: THE AGENDA*

In international dealings, well-designed agendas are useful even when they are unnatural in the local context. Circular agendas, and oblique approaches to problems are fine if the communication between parties is subtle and highly developed. Often, however, there is some communication difficulty – language being the obvious example. In these cases overt, straight-line agendas are best. They reduce anxiety and promote understanding and free the mind to concentrate on what is important.

# EXERCISE

You are setting up a meeting with a partner you know quite well, to discuss a bundle of issues. You are free to decide the running order of the following.

A.  A point of technical detail with no immediate repercussions.
B.  Some long-term thoughts you've been wanting to air.

---

\* Nemawashi: the process of consultation so essential to Japanese decision making.

C.   A delicate item, difficult to agree on.
D.   Immediate action points.
E.   Good news for your partner.
F.   A matter to be agreed, probably quickly and easily.
G.   Bad news for your partner

Think about it for a moment. Then write down the seven letters, in the running order you would favour:

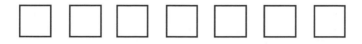

Now take a look at our version in Appendix 5B, at the end of this chapter.

### THE AGENDA IS ON THE TABLE. IS THE AGENDA ON THE TABLE?

The expression 'hidden agenda' has become fashionable lately. We have heard it used as a synonym for 'ulterior motive', as in 'He asked me back to his place for coffee, but I think he had a hidden agenda.'

We use the term as follows: your *hidden agenda* is the list of items in order of *importance* for you and your side. It might include some items which do not appear on the *open agenda*, which is the list of discussion points for the meeting, in order of *time*.

### HOW TO HANDLE TWO AGENDAS

The banker's priorities differ from his client's, the salesperson's from his purchaser's, the HQ man's from the country manager's, the boss's from the employee's. Contrasting cultures will make such differences even greater. Hidden agendas diverge.

Wonderful. If they ran parallel and close, never touching, there would be few opportunities for creative trade and exchange. So:

### Clarify your own hidden agenda

Dig deeper into your own needs and desires. Perhaps you have been carried along by circumstances so fast that you have lost touch with your own, or your organization's, purpose. Be sure you know what really matters and what doesn't. This is especially important if you are negotiating as part of a team.

**And theirs**

Write down in note form everything you've gathered or guessed about their priorities. Shuffle your notes around to get a proper feeling for their needs.

**Agree an open agenda first**

This can often be done before the meeting (one of the best uses of e-mail or the fax machine), with some fine tuning once the meeting begins – 'Are we sure this agenda suits us both?' The purpose is not to impose discipline or save time, but to build confidence, demonstrate common interests, and open the road to agreement on matters of substance.

**Allow time for exploration**

Two ways of looking at the situation:

- My company has spent a lot of money flying me out here, so I must make sure no time is wasted, which means getting down to practicalities as quickly as we can. No time for waffle.

- My company has spent a lot of money flying me out here, so I must make sure we do the job properly, which means sounding out the other side thoroughly before we get down to practicalities. Otherwise we shall inevitably miss opportunities, and I might as well have stayed at home.

**Then start trading**

You can give something away that is insignificant on *your* hidden agenda, but more important to *him*. In return, he yields to you on a minor matter to him which is vital to you. You both finish with a gain at the cost of something trivial.

---

*A NON-WESTERN VIEW OF AGENDAS*

To me, as an Arab, drawing an agenda is a very Western thing. It attempts to compensate Westerners for their short and limited memories. A hidden agenda allows me the flexibility to drop certain issues if I feel that the time is not right for them. Equally, I find that written agendas will force a linear progression, which is impersonal, rigid and possibly confrontational. The hidden circular approach allows me the ability to duck and dive, to surprise my counterpart, and to divert any potential confrontation. What I like is to be able to approach the meeting in a holistic way, to spend some time discussing everything and nothing, to get the feel of my counterpart, his mood and temperament, his eagerness and readiness, before I launch into business. As a high context person, I do not like the Western reductionist approach that tries to do one thing at a time, it is also so monochronic. I suppose it is good in the scientific and engineering spheres, but it is not creative.

Dr Jehad Al-Omari, Canning consultant

## APPENDIX 5A – WHICH NATIONALITY WAS THE OBJECT OF EACH COMMENT?

1. The Swedes

2. A Frenchman (who worked for an American company)

3. A Frenchman (who worked for a state-run bureaucracy)

4. The Japanese

5. The British

6. The Finns

7. The Italians

8. The Swiss

9. The Americans

10. The Germans

## APPENDIX 5B – THE AGENDA GAME

E. Good news first promotes a positive atmosphere. Anyway, to withhold it seems artificial.

G. Bad news next to get it out of the way. Again, keeping it until later in the meeting seems manipulative.

F. Easy negotiations now, to re-establish the lost momentum.

B. Long-term ideas, unlikely to spark conflict, establish a sense of trust to put the next item in context.

C.  Delicate item.
A.  Minor technical matter can be postponed if time runs short.
D.  Immediate action points, likely to be affected by the foregoing, so keep them until last – where they are also likely to be remembered.

Cultural variation? We have found a tendency among North Europeans to deliver the bad news early – perhaps out of Lutheran honesty. Managers in more relaxed cultures often put item D first – for fear it might be forgotten.

# 6

# Talk

Talk is the point of contact. Speak clearly and listen closely, and agreement becomes possible. To be clear and convincing in the international arena requires special skills.

Talking and listening, at the sharp end of our pyramid, happen in real time. All your careful preparation can be wasted if the message is distorted at the moment of contact. So it is a good idea to do a little work on your message in advance. What sort of work do we mean?

In this chapter we will lead you to an understanding of how to shape your message to cross barriers of culture and language.

## A WORLD LANGUAGE?

When Alexander the Great died in 323 BC, his empire collapsed into bickering factions. They all bickered in *Greek*. A common form of Greek remained as the language of the Eastern Mediterranean for more than 1000 years.

The Roman legions marched across Western Europe, built their great straight roads, and spread the *Latin* language. When the Vandals ripped the heart out of the Empire (455 AD), the roads and the language remained. As the roads crumbled away, the soldiers' dialect of Latin evolved into the Romance languages – French, Spanish, Portuguese, Romanian. Latin itself lived on as the language of the Roman church and the educated elite ('the ghost of the Roman Empire, sitting crowned upon the grave thereof', Gibbon). Until the Reformation, church Latin was standard from Bohemia to Ireland, and from Stockholm to Cadiz. Another empire was built by the conquistadors in Central and South America. Linguistically, it lives on; today over 200 million people outside Spain speak Spanish as their first language – a direct descendent of Latin in lands the Legions never knew.

The *Arabic* language travelled with Islam around the Southern Mediterranean. Today, Arabic speakers outside the Arabian peninsula outnumber Saudi Arabians by 15 to 1.

In the 18th and 19th centuries, the intellectual and political prestige of France made *French* a contender for the title of 'World Language'. Educated people throughout the world learned French as their first foreign language: the Russian aristocracy spoke it in preference to Russian.

*German*, too, came close to being a lingua franca. As German merchants and settlers established a network throughout Central Europe, from the early middle ages to the industrial revolution, theirs was the language of trade. (There is a widespread myth that German was nearly adopted as the language of the infant US – that the proposal was defeated by just one vote in Congress. But it is only a myth.)

Being a lingua franca means much more than just the fact that 'a lot of people speak it'. *Standard Chinese* has the greatest number of native speakers in the world, and yet is understood and used by virtually nobody outside the native-speaking community.

So far, no other language has spread as far as *English*. Three factors have set English up as the world language: Empire, the Merchant Navy, and the computer.

- *Empire* left a string of English-speaking settlements in relatively empty lands such as Australia, New Zealand, Canada and the US. In more populous territories, such as India and Africa, the English language has outlasted Empire as the most convenient way to talk between communities. (There are at least 500 distinct languages in sub-Saharan Africa, and even more in the Indian sub-continent.) Today, English is an official language in 45 different countries, from Anguilla to Zimbabwe.

- During the British dominance of world trade in the 19th century, the *Merchant Navy* established the island's language, often in crude form, as the most reliable way to have a cargo loaded or unloaded in almost any port in the world. As British trade declined, the Americans moved in, speaking the same language – more or less.

- Thanks to the US dominance of the *computer* industry in its early days, English provides the vocabulary for describing the machines and the jobs they do. As the great dictionaries of the world's languages appear in new editions and supplements, many of the new usages they list are in the area of computer science, and most of those usages spring from English.

## A LANGUAGE FOR BUSINESS

Shell, the Anglo-Dutch company, chose English as its language in the 1920s. After all, how many of the British managers spoke Dutch?

By the 1970s, it seemed natural that Chancellor Schmidt and President Giscard d'Estaing, building European unity, should talk to each other in fluent English, even if the British were absent from the table.

When, in the late 1980s, Swedish ASEA and Swiss Brown Boveri became ABB, English was again the language of convenience – a language both Swedish and Swiss engineers could handle.

As the old regimes of Eastern Europe tumbled in 1989–90, and the new popular movements showed themselves to the world on television, there was always an English speaker on hand to address the microphones.

Similar instances abound. To speak in English is to speak to the world. The language has cut loose its moorings to the island of its origin.

As a French businessman put it: 'The English language does not belong to the British, you know.'

## ENGLISH IN THE WORLD TODAY

- 300 million speak English as their mother tongue;

- 800 million more put it to use daily;

- 75 per cent of the world's mail is in English; as are

- 80 per cent of the data stored on the world's computers, and

- 45 per cent of the world's scientific publications.

The use of English is growing geometrically, and will probably only be limited by the number of people in the world. The need for a world language has never been so great.

## ARTIFICIAL LANGUAGES

Of course, there have also been attempts to *create* a world language. Esperanto, the best-known artificial language, was invented in the 1880s. Twenty years ago, the Esperanto Society claimed eight million speakers in 100 countries. Its advocates claim that the administrative life of the UN/the EC/the Olympic Committee would be transformed by the adoption of Esperanto. Their arguments, usually presented in English, fall on deaf ears.

In the 1930s a group of linguists and intellectuals promoted 'Basic English', which trims the excess richness of English vocabulary, and irons out the more complex folds of its grammar.

(In fact, derivatives of Basic English are quite widely used in technical documentation, to avoid confusion arising from the sloppy use of synonyms: 'switch', 'button', 'knob', 'rocker', 'control', 'lever', 'contact', 'relay' and so on.)

Two forces work against artificially created languages. First, language is by its nature a slippery and undisciplined creature. The Académie in France is the object of wry amusement as it tries to keep the French language pure, and to stop the French people saying just what they feel like saying. Marcel insists on his right to go 'footing' and drop off his 'smoking' at the 'pressing' ('jogging', 'dinner jacket', and 'dry cleaner's'). Any language designed by academics has only a slim chance of survival.

The second factor is a matter of headcount and investment. It is a long job, learning a language. From a zero start, the average adult must spend several hundred hours in dedicated study before he can hold even a straightforward conversation on an undemanding topic with a sympathetic partner. Hobbyists apart, such an effort is only worth while if there are lots of other people around with whom to speak the language.

---

**DEFINITIONS**

*First language, native language, mother tongue:* one learnt in childhood, and so the one in which the speaker normally thinks – whence 'native speaker'.

*Dialect:* a regional variant of a standard language in which grammar, vocabulary and accent are markedly different, but still comprehensible to the main community.

*Patois:* a dialect spoken in a small isolated region – eg, mountain villages.

*Pidgin:* (corruption of the word 'business') a way of speaking which mixes two or more languages together – typically by laying vocabulary from one over the grammar of another. Common in

---

the Pacific, where English and Chinese mix. (*'Baiim Namba Wan Wailis!'* ('Buy the best radio!') – Sony slogan.

*Creole:* a pidgin which has become a mother tongue. The vernacular of New Orleans is an example (probably from Portuguese *crioulo* – home-born slave).

*Artificial language:* one created by linguistic specialists.

*Natural language:* one created by its users over time.

*Lingua franca:* 'mixture of Italian with French, Greek, Arabic, and Spanish, used in the Levant; any language serving as medium between different nations whose own languages are not the same; system providing mutual understanding. [It = Frankish tongue]' (*Concise Oxford Dictionary*)

*Standard English:* (henceforward SE): the English language as spoken by native speakers, including varieties from America, Australia, etc.

*Offshore English:* (offshore, or OE): our own term for the English language as spoken by people with other first languages, who have learnt it as adults, for practical rather than academic purposes.

## OFFSHORE ENGLISH–LANGUAGE OF CONVENIENCE

In the rest of this book we will describe how Offshore English is used as an effective tool in international business. It is aimed in two directions at once.

- First, if you are a native speaker of English, we give guidance on how to modify your way of speaking. As a master of the language, you have the primary responsibility for the communication channel. It is you who must ensure that it is clean and free of extraneous noise.

- Second, if you are a non-native speaker, we suggest how you can make the maximum impact in English, and where you should concentrate your efforts as you work for improvement.

For both, we point out some of the common causes of misunderstanding.

In the *Cambridge Encyclopedia of Language*, David Crystal lays down six criteria for evaluating an international language. He had in mind artificial languages, but the questions raised are a valid test for this 'evolved' language.

## 1. EASY TO LEARN

For the 310 million native speakers of Standard English, Offshore English should be easy enough – requiring less investment of time and effort than a completely foreign language. That said, they have a poor record generally in communicating outside their own language group. There are skills involved in high-level Offshore which Standard speakers sadly ignore. More of that later in this chapter.

For outsiders, English grammar is comparatively easy in the early stages – and Offshore goes little further than the early stages. There are no case or gender problems with nouns or adjectives ('The young man meets the young woman', and vice versa), and few verb changes ('I walked, you walked, they walked'). On the other hand, English spelling is a disaster area.

## 2. RELATABLE TO MOTHER TONGUES

Since English is a hybrid of Germanic and Latinate strains, there is some case of access for Continental neighbours, Latin Americans, and francophone Africans. There are many points of contact in vocabulary, eg:

| German | Fleisch | →Flesh |
| Italian | Societa | →Society |
| Swedish | Fisk | →Fish |
| French | Chambre | →Chamber |

Further afield, but within the Indo-European language family:

| Greek | Kyklos | →Cycle |
| Russian | Voda | →Water |
| Persian | Dokhtar | →Daughter |
| Hindi | Raj | →Royalty |

For Hungarians, Finns, Japanese and others the going is tougher.

## 3. A RICH RANGE OF FUNCTIONS

Offshore has evolved through use and has no set limits. Pop songs and papal blessings, table tennis tournaments and train timetables – all can be handled in Offshore. If not, Offshore expands until they can, drawing on the wealth of Standard English.

## 4. STANDARDIZED

Not yet. There is no authority to press it into a single mould. Yet the forces that have brought it into being are still at work on it, and will tend to bring about harmonization and homogeneity. We predict a world in which a fairly universal Offshore is spoken, wherever administrators, technicians and tourists gather. But at home with their families they will continue to use Georgian or Geordie.

The Dutch and many Scandinavians already live this way. Fluent in English for all practical tasks, they keep their real mother tongue for more intimate or local concerns.

## 5. NEUTRAL

Offshore scores rather badly here. There are many who resent the world dominance of English, either because of a colonial past, or because they would like the world to be speaking Offshore French, Offshore German or whatever. Native Standard speakers should tread carefully, and never abuse their apparent advantage.

Margaret Thatcher visited Madrid in May 1989, and her schedule included a meeting with a senior minister who spoke excellent English. They had met before. High-level gossip in Spain was that he insisted on working through an interpreter the second time. The reason? At their previous meeting, the story went, Mrs Thatcher had used cricket talk ('sticky wicket' and 'bowl him a googly', presumably) in order to assert her dominance in the conversation.

We hope the story is not true; the important thing is that it was being told. As Spain has emerged into the European and global market, many Spaniards have had to work very hard to catch up in Offshore English (French being the traditional foreign language at school in Spain) and, like many in the world, they take it unkindly when they meet a Brit, American or Australian who seems to be taking unfair advantage.

Incidentally, not everybody sees it as an advantage. An Italian businessman says:

> I feel sorry for the British manager: he can never be truly European. Let me give you an example. If I go to, say, Denmark, then what language do I choose? . . . English, of course. Just as it is when the British manager goes. The crucial difference is, when I go there, I have to stop being Italian . . .

## 6. PROVIDING INSIGHT

Some creators of artificial languages had aspirations to clarifying human thought. A logical language would make people think more logically. Mathematics is the only 'language' that can show results in this direction. Unfortunately, mathematics will not help you get a drink at a crowded bar.

Learning a 'real' foreign language is a way of gaining insight, and broadening your perspectives. The dominance of Offshore means that many native speakers of Standard English do not bother. That is their loss. An English businessman looking across at Europe (for him England is not in 'Europe'):

> They've all got a *natural advantage* over us, haven't they? I mean, they all speak English already. How many of us speak German or Spanish or whatever? It hardly seems right somehow.

### Message for native speakers of English

Murphy's Law, as it applies to language in international business, states: 'When you have spent 500 hours of your precious time learning the rudiments of Business French, then and only then will the board post you to Dusseldorf.'

You would do better to spend a little time learning to speak Offshore. It is a more useful instrument than school French, school German, or the English you speak at home.

## WHY ENGLISH HURTS

Every language has its own special tortures for the learner. Slovene has not only singular and plural, but also a special set of *dual* forms. In Hungarian, to say 'in' Budapest, Eger or any other Hungarian town requires different grammatical forms from those needed to say 'in' Detroit, Bogota, or any town anywhere else. A Korean places his listener in one of six social gradings when he chooses a verb suffix.

This section consists of seven sketches of various painful aspects of Standard English that might not have occurred to you if you are a native speaker. We hope to encourage you to be more sympathetic to those who have learnt it from zero, to be more tolerant of their mistakes, and perhaps to modify your own way of talking.

## 1. TIME

Every student of English-as-a-foreign-language will agree: the correct use of verb tenses is one of the biggest headaches. No other language makes quite the same distinctions between 'He smokes' and 'He's smoking', between 'I smoked for years' and 'I've been smoking for years'. There are several extra colours in the English rainbow, it seems, when verbs and time meet.

But verbs are not the only tricky area. The distinction between 'by next Friday' and 'until next Friday' is elusive, as is the exact difference between 'finally' and 'at last'. 'Already', 'yet', 'just', 'still', 'always', 'again', 'before', 'ago' – all are much more difficult to handle than 'cup and saucer' or 'joint venture'. Unconscious slips are frequent.

The wise user of Offshore always double-checks when time is an issue: 'Can we just verify all dates and deadlines? . . .'

## 2. PARTS OF SPEECH

Newspaper headlines in English often confuse foreigners, even when the topic is well known to them. One reason lies in a trick peculiar to English: the self-same word can often be an adjective or a noun.

So 'bus' is definitely a noun, until we use it in the phrase 'bus driver', when it serves as an adjective. Consider the headline 'Chicago bus driver pension plan dispute announcement.'

Confusion can arise between 'price list' and 'list price'.

Conversely, a word first met as a verb – I sleep, we copy, they read – can also appear as a noun – refreshing sleep, illegible copy, a good read.

## 3. PREPOSITIONS AND OTHER LITTLE WORDS

Prepositions are a bit of a lottery in many languages. When the dictionary tells you that *na* in Russian means 'on', that doesn't mean you are right to say *na* Friday, or *na* target.

English often presents a difficult choice, using two different words where one serves both purposes in the Offshore user's home language. In German, *seit* covers 'for 65 years' and 'since 1934'.

## 4. CONTRACTIONS

The conversational habit of contracting 'I am going' into 'I'm going' can be tiring for the Offshore listener, but it is generally understood.

There is one notable danger: the contraction of 'cannot' into 'can't' (especially with a short New York 'a'). A sentence like 'I can't tell you the result before Friday' is easily misheard as 'I can tell you . . .'

## 5. REGISTER

Simply put, choosing the right 'register' in a language means selecting the appropriate expressions and tone of voice for a given situation – and more particularly for the person to whom you are talking. So there is one way of asking your teenage son to pass the salt and quite another for the First Lady.

Modern English uses the word 'you' for both the polite form of address and the familiar ('thou' died some time ago). Native speakers compensate by using 'could you possibly' or 'perhaps you might' when they are on their best behaviour. When they choose the imperative ('Close the door behind you!'), they use subtle inflections of voice to avoid sounding like a sergeant major. Such nuances are not easy for an outsider to master.

A Portuguese person speaking to a Greek in Offshore will save time and effort by simplifying his register. The Greek is not likely to take offence, so long as there's a smile. Native speakers sometimes take offence unnecessarily.

The English themselves have an international reputation as word-mincers. A memorandum from London headquarters which begins 'You might like to consider revising your plans . . .' can cause total confusion, even in North America: is this a suggestion? a proposal? an instruction? The French traditionally refer to Britain as 'Perfidious Albion'. British talents for acting and espionage are well recognized, and the reputation is confirmed by the habit of prefacing any form of pressure with a softener: 'I wonder if you could possibly replace these faulty goods'; 'Terribly sorry, but you're in breach of contract'. 'Economical with the truth' is a phrase which illustrates so well what it describes.

## 6. CONNECTORS

In conversation, native speakers usually restrict themselves to a short list of simple connectors: 'We were hoping to launch the product in April, but there was a transport strike, so we missed the launch date by a month.'

Offshore speakers often favour more literary or legalistic methods of coupling up their ideas: 'however' and 'therefore' are stronger and clearer than 'but', and 'so'. 'Moreover', 'nevertheless', 'consequently', 'as follows' and 'with regard to' do not feel pompous in spoken Offshore.

## 7. OBLIGATION

There are quite subtle shades of meaning between 'You mustn't drink and drive' and 'You don't have to do military service' – not to mention 'You don't have to be an expert to see that this is a fake', or 'You really must visit us next time you're in Seattle'.

Offshore users often stumble. Again, it is a good idea to double-check when listening, and use less elusive forms – 'necessary' and 'possible' – when speaking.

### TEST (for native speakers of English)

In the best tradition of school language primers, we offer native speakers of Standard English a test:

Translate the following into Offshore, trying to retain as much as possible of the original message, while accepting some loss of flavour:

1. It can hardly have escaped your attention that our competitors have been stealing a march on us of late.

2. Short of taking him out and shooting him, I don't see how we'll ever get shot of him.

3. Far be it from me to teach you how to suck eggs, but are you quite sure you're tackling the issue the right way?

4. I wouldn't for a moment want you to think I'm uninterested in what I half-guess you're about to say, but could I get a word in edgeways before you get rolling?

5. You took your time! What kept you?

Answers in Appendix 6A, at the end of this chapter.

## HOW TO USE OFFSHORE ENGLISH

### 1. GRADE YOUR LANGUAGE

> You tell me this is a popular newspaper – a paper for ordinary people. Why do I find it more difficult to read than *The Economist?*
> Frenchman brandishing an English tabloid

English is an idiomatic language. An idiom enriches a language, but also presents a barrier.

'It's no use crying over spilt milk' is a proverb, not an idiom. The use of proverbs in Offshore can be irritating, partly because they use local cultural references ('Penny wise, pound foolish'), and partly because they often contain problem words. So the use of 'Too many cooks spoil the broth' leads to tedious explanations of 'broth', which is a rare word known to very few outsiders; the alternative is to say 'Too many cooks spoil the soup'.

'We must grasp the bull by the horns' is a cliche now, but in its younger days it was a vigorous figure of speech, a metaphor. Metaphors are fine in Offshore – again provided they contain no mystifying words. The advanced student of Offshore is often tempted to make his language more colourful by learning a battery of metaphorical cliches, but there are dangers. 'A finger in every pie' can easily slip and become 'A finger in every tart'. We promise this is a real example.*

The English idioms that cause learners most serious problems involve the use of a handful of verbs – *be, have, do, make, go, put, take* and, above all, *get*, together with a longer list of adverbs and prepositions – *up, down, in, around, after, by, for, with, from, to, at, across, over, under, out, along . . .*

After a hard day, the husband had been instructed by his concerned wife to sit down and relax for an hour with the evening newspaper while she fixed dinner. He was feeling fidgety, and she caught him on the way to the kitchen:

'What are you up to?'

'I'm just going to wash the salad . . .'

'Are you up to it?'

'Of course I am.'

'Well, it's up to you.'

This is also a real example. It translates into Offshore as follows:

'What are you doing?' (in a suspicious tone of voice).

'I'm just going to wash the salad . . .'

'But you're tired. Are you sure?'

'Of course I am.'

'Well, it's your decision.'

So the native speaker of Standard English, which is saturated with such expressions, must learn to edit them out of his speech if he wants to communicate smoothly with other members of the Offshore club.

Setting aside the tricky idioms for a moment, we move on to the question of pure vocabulary. Our third real example:

Klaus Weisse was a student on a language course. By standard measurements, his English was 'low intermediate', although by using punchy Offshore he was capable of getting any job done on the oil-rig where he worked. An English visitor to his college was introduced to him, and the director of studies invited Klaus to comment on the quality of the course. 'Speak your mind, Klaus,' said the visitor, 'Don't be a creep.'

'Creep' is a rare word. It means, usually, 'to move with the body horizontal and close to the ground', and Offshore only uses the word if zoologists are conversing. So Klaus had probably never met it.

He had certainly never met it in the sense of 'a person who creeps, fig-

---

* Note for non-native speakers: 'He has a finger in every pie' means 'He is involved in every aspect of business'; a pie and a tart are very similar in the kitchen, but 'tart' is also a colloquial term for 'prostitute'.

uratively, in the presence of superiors'. Anyway, the English preparatory school idea of 'creeping to teacher' is confined to that culture.

To make matters worse, the English visitor in question was using irony – he didn't really mean what he was saying. Irony is very dangerous in Offshore contexts. So all in all, Klaus had very little chance of coming up with a suitable riposte.

He just looked blank and rather sad.

## 2. USE THE FULL RANGE OF TONE AND TEMPO

'Well, that was certainly the longest report I've ever written.'

English is a tonal language – much more so than many of its Continental neighbours. A large part of the message is encoded in the way an utterance is delivered, so the sentence above can have several distinct meanings, according to where you place the emphasis, where you pause, and where your voice rises and falls.

Any outsider who has studied English by enlightened methods, or who has had real exposure to living English in his working or social life, is conscious of this. Some manage to reproduce the sound patterns accurately, and to use this extra dimension when they communicate. Others – less musically inclined, perhaps – import the tone systems from their own language.

Whether or not he 'sounds English', your Offshore partner will be sensitive to a greater or lesser extent to the tonal nuances he hears. One significant difference between good and bad speakers of Offshore is this: the good ones use a wide range of tone and tempo to strengthen their messages, while the bad ones sound flat and monotonous.

### A message for everybody

Place stress on the key words, and punch your message out. After all, there is something in the nature of English that lends itself to the rhythms of rock music. Lennon and McCartney's classic world hits were written and recorded in Offshore – simple, direct language delivered with great effect.

Make greater use of significant pauses, giving your audience time to digest what you have just said, creating an appetite for what you are about to say.

### Message for Standard English native speakers

Use natural intonation and breath-grouping.

Ifyou*speak* . . . like*this* . . . and*put*abitta*music* . . . intowhaty-ou*say* . . . your*part*nercan*fol*low . . . much*bet*ter.

It is harder for him to understand the loud-flat-delivery-of-evenly-spaced-words-one-at-a-time.

When you want to make a point clearly, you will naturally tend to slow down. Try to achieve the effect . . . by chopping your sentence . . . into idea-groups . . ., pausing after each.

Your listeners have been trained, either formally or by experience, to understand the contractions of spoken English – 'Now we're gonna decide who's responsible for the contract they've signed'. You run a serious risk of sounding patronising (the 'Watch My Lips' syndrome) if you slow down too much, and say 'Now we are going to decide who is responsible for the contract they have signed.' So don't.

## Message for OE speakers

Do not make the mistake of confusing speed with fluency. As you make progress in English, there is a temptation to demonstrate your skill by speaking more quickly. Resist it.

## 3. ACCENTUATE THE POSITIVE

> 'It isn't that I'm suggesting you couldn't solve the problem, but . . .'

A native speaker can take this sort of construction in his stride – perhaps. Any other listener goes into mental spasm for a moment – are you saying he can solve the problem, or the opposite? What was that old rule he learned at school about two negatives making an affirmative? What are you going to say next, and will he be able to keep up?

These intricate sets of negatives, nested one inside the other like Russian dolls, are typical of Standard English (the language of diplomacy) but very damaging in Offshore. If you catch yourself uttering one – and the momentary panic in your partner's eyes should alert you – stop and say: 'Sorry, that wasn't very clear . . . We all know you *could* solve the problem, but . . .'

> 'If we don't invest in this plant, we won't be able to meet demand next year.'

Statements like this are bad salesmanship. They create depressing pictures in the listener's mind. People respond more willingly to promises than to threats. Try: 'If we invest in this plant, we'll be in a good position to meet demand . . .'

> 'Not a bad effort. Not bad at all.'

Standard English, especially the British version, depends on complex patterns of understatement, irony and nuance of tone. Such mannerisms are often misunderstood in Offshore, and can cause disappointment or worse. If somebody performs well, say 'Well done. Excellent.'

## 4. SHOW WARMTH; SHOW WILLINGNESS

Cultural embarrassment, and lack of language subtlety, can put a brake on friendliness. Sad to relate, acquaintance in international business often stops short at 'How was your flight? Good, let's get down to business', or 'Of course you know him. Big guy. Glasses. Works in Treasury in Minnesota.'

Warm and lasting relationships will be at a premium in the business world of the future; people are tired of 'Wham-Bam-Thank You, Ma'am'. If you want to stand out in the crowd, as a person interested in people, make use of social time and small talk to go a little deeper – as we suggested back in Chapter 3. How?

- By asking questions, *listening* to the answers, and asking supplementary questions:
  'Are you from a big family? What does/did your father do?'
  'Are you a city or country person at heart? If you had your choice, where would you live?'
  'Are you a good cook? Specialities? Secrets?'

- By letting out a little more about yourself, as a signal that your partner can talk freely about himself.

- By remembering that nearly everybody's favourite subject of conversation, finally, is himself.

In language terms, Offshore is sometimes a little curt:
  'Are you in pharmaceuticals?'
  'Yes.'
  'Who do you work for?'
  'Novartis.'
Standard English uses echoing devices to create reciprocal warmth:
  'Are you in pharmaceuticals?'
  'Yes, I am.'
  'Really? Who do you work for?'
  'For Novartis.'

The trick is to *give more than the minimum* and *mirror your partner's tone*.

In our own culture, we often rely on subtle indicators to display or detect enthusiasm – particularly tone of voice – and are afraid of seeming naive or ingenuous. Across language barriers, or in the neutral territory of Offshore, unspoken signals rarely work. State your good intentions overtly, and state them often:
  'This will help both of us.'
  'I'd really like to hear more about that.'
  'We're very keen to reach agreement on this.'

## 5. USE QUESTIONS TO GOOD EFFECT

Sometimes there's no better way of making a point than by asking a question – is there? And who knows that better than the seasoned professional communicator – the politician, the barrister, the advertising man?

The salesman in particular understands the power of the 'Yes-sequence':

'Now you're a businessman, aren't you?'

'Yes.'

'Can I assume you're always interested in ways of reducing your overheads?'

'Yes.'

'Do you sometimes worry about the size of your telephone bill?'

'Yes.'

'Will you buy this patent telephone bill reducer?'

'Yes.'

The technique has value in every language. Most business people, operating in their native languages, recognize that value.

Yet transactions in Offshore often get stuck in the rut of statement and counter-statement.

### Message to Offshore speakers

There are two probable reasons why you do not use enough questions.

- The formation of questions in English is difficult.

- Your language habitually uses 'statement forms' to ask questions: 'You are Signor Rossi?'; 'It's time to start the meeting?'.

Try this: next time you are going to a meeting, think in advance of the two or three points you want to make. Write them down using ten words for each. Now translate each into a question: 'Can anybody here see a real alternative?'; 'What have we learned from last year's poor results?'; 'How many of our big customers today were small customers five years ago?'. Use those questions to make your points at the meeting. The habit will grow on you.

### Message to SE native speakers

Your interlocutor is under pressure in many ways. English grammar is not so straightforward as you assume. Questions can cause headaches. There are the mysteries of auxiliaries and modals (do, have, will, would, etc): 'What do cannibals eat? Who do cannibals eat? What eats cannibals? Who eats cannibals?'

There are nested questions: 'Don't you think; we should stop wondering why we didn't do well last time, and start thinking about who can do what to make sure we do do well next time?'

When you ask a question of an Offshore speaker, make sure your question is simple enough to be answerable. Then check that the answer is an answer to the question you asked.

## 6. KEEP IT SHORT AND SIMPLE – SOMETIMES

When people are being trained to make presentations, they are often exhorted to 'Keep It Short and Simple' (KISS).

If they are SE speakers preparing for an SE audience, KISS often means opting for Saxon vocabulary – 'feed' rather than 'nourish', 'target' rather than 'objective', 'dream' rather than 'fantasize'. Hamlet's 'To be or not to be?' works better than 'I am confronted by an existential dilemma'.

However, if your Offshore audience includes a contingent from a Romance language base, the advice should be different. Their ears and minds are conditioned to process longer, more Latinate words more easily. Everyday conversation in Italy, Spain and France is peppered with words that seem abstract or high-flown.

So 'We didn't sell as many as we'd hoped, I'm afraid' gives a Venezuelan listener trouble. More Latin would be: 'Unfortunately, our revenue was inferior to our predictions.' This is ugly by any standards, and good Offshore strikes a compromise with something like 'Unfortunately, we didn't reach our sales objective'.

The other part of the KISS principle – one idea per sentence – holds true in any language. 'Because it was her grandmother's birthday and in spite of the dangers of the forest, Little Red Riding Hood, who was a good little girl . . .' is poor stuff. And in case you think it only happens in badly told fairy stories, here is an anonymous example from an in-house sales document:

> 'Whereas each of these considerations treated in isolation may appear to be of minor importance, they will when totalled together make a useful contribution to overall cost reduction.'

Try chopping that one up into digestible pieces.

## 7. USE BIG, BOLD SIGNPOSTS

We have more than once in the last three chapters, made the point that a clear framework or agenda is essential for effective communication across cultures. Your travelling companion will relax and enjoy the trip if he knows the length and direction of the journey, and how many halts there will be for refreshment and exercise.

Markers, placed along the way, offer reassurance. Between native speakers of the same language, they are often brief and subtle. Indeed, it is considered rather pedestrian to sign off each point formally ('And that is all I have to say regarding the second item') before moving on ('so it is clearly time to turn our attention to item number three').

Offshore is not afraid to be pedestrian occasionally, especially if clarity and security are at stake. 'So much for X, let's move on to Y'; 'That covers production, so what about sales?'; 'Turning from Japan to Korea . . .'; 'I think we're ready now to change the subject . . .' – such deliberate and obvious 'discourse markers' make for harmony and control.

Native speakers of any language cut corners or jump over gaps when they are in a hurry. Standard English typically omits relative pronouns and conjunctions, and this can be worrying to the Offshore listener. 'I told the salesman you sent the prices he quoted were too high' is a bit of a strain for somebody whose native language would always use several extra words in such a sentence: 'I told the salesman *whom* you sent *that* the prices *which* he quoted were too high.' Not surprisingly, Offshore English tends to point up the grammatical relationships in each sentence.

## 8. SUMMARIZE OFTEN

There is an old saying about public speaking: 'Tell them what you're going to say; say it; tell them what you've said'. Again, it sounds a bit repetitive and unexciting. Professional comics don't do that, do they? And magicians pull rabbits out of hats without all that tedious explanation. If you are a comic or a magician, carry on. For the rest of us, it is a good idea to learn to walk before we try to run.

Everybody at the meeting will love you if, from time to time, you provide a neat summary of the action so far. To be the summarizer gives you power: you are effectively deciding what the meeting has achieved so far. Your summary should be unambiguous, fair and immediately comprehensible to all present. Otherwise it will be worse than useless and everybody will hate you.

Remember that your summary should be shorter than the material you are summarizing – unlike many we have heard.

## 9. DON'T WORRY ABOUT BODY LANGUAGE

Television programmes, handbooks and training courses which touch on 'personal communication' often dwell on body language, emphasizing areas of difference between cultures: Sicilian males embrace, while Swedish males do not; it is wrong to show the soles of your feet to an Arab; never touch the head of a Thai; and so on.

People are fascinated, because the messages are directed at a human weak spot – insecurity about how others perceive us. But the advice and the warnings can have a damaging effect. The 'communicator' enters his next transaction nervous of making a mistake, and the proceedings become stiff and unnatural.

Charles Darwin, the earliest scientific investigator into non-verbal communication, came to the conclusion: 'All the chief expressions exhibited by man are the same throughout the world.' That was in 1872.

In today's business world, just as Offshore English is penetrating everywhere, so there are standards in body language that are universally recognized.

● When you meet your partner *on neutral territory*, the universal code should be enough: smile, firm handshake, steady eye-contact, relaxed but dignified bearing.

● *On your own territory*, point out any major gaffes to them ('In Japan, we show great respect to the business card . . .'), but otherwise be as flexible towards them as you would expect them to be with you.

● On their territory, find an opportunity to observe how people carry themselves and approach each other. Hotel lobbies are a good place. Then, if there is anything noticeably different, consider adapting your own style for the sake of harmony. But do nothing that might seem artificial or clumsy. Your Offshore partner wants you to relax and be yourself.

Much of the communication between you will happen at a level deeper than words. Part of the purpose of meetings, of business travel, is to establish trusting relationships. How can your partner trust you if you are trying to be something you are not?

> One can lie with the mouth, but with the accompanying grimace one nevertheless tells the truth.
>
> Nietzsche

## 10. ADD A LITTLE SPICE

Offshore is not a language for writing great comedies or tragedies. Yet its most effective practitioners manage to be lively and stimulating.

*Jokes*, the rehearsed sort that begin 'Have you heard the one about . . .?', should be used with care. The great majority depend for their humorous effect on some cultural or linguistic twist that does not travel well. If you find yourself in a joke-swopping session, the most workable are short, simple jokes about universal human foibles. The classic targets are avarice (the Scots, the Schwaben, and the Auvergnats have been very patient) and stupidity (an endless list of victims here – check the local scene). If you can avoid any suggestion of racism or sexism your listeners will be more comfortable. Self-deprecation, and the deprecation of your own culture, are welcome (and the best Jewish jokes are told by Jews).

That said, we are all in favour of *humour*, as is the Offshore business community at large. *Anecdotes* often work better than set-piece jokes, especially if they are about the Offshore world: 'Do you know, I was checking out of a hotel in Djakarta a few weeks ago, and . . .'

When you have time to plan what you are going to say – a presentation, perhaps – you have the opportunity to design your message for maximum impact and memorability. Few of us are advertising copywriters, but most of us can rise to a little 'colourful speech', and in the Offshore world it counts for a lot.

*Images and analogies* are already present in large numbers in the basic business vocabulary: hands-on experience; turnkey projects; golden handshakes; and the product launch. All these are so familiar that the original image no longer comes to life in the mind of the listener; they are clichés. One fresh image within your presentation will work wonders: 'Think of it as a . . .'; 'This reminds me of that familiar moment when . . .'; 'We've all had the experience, at one time or another, of . . .'. As with humour, make sure the image you are suggesting 'translates' into your listener's world. For example: in Western cultures, mice love cheese. In Eastern countries with no dairy tradition, they are more likely to be grain thieves. Talk of 'bread-and-butter projects', 'cash-cow products', and 'creaming-off of profits' is also likely to confuse.

*Rhyme and alliteration* work perfectly well: 'vision and decision'; 'are we going to tell him the idea, or sell him the idea?'; 'product, price and positioning.' The non-native speaker enjoys grasping items of word-play and passing them on to others.

*The personal touch* is also important. 'Sales of the soft drink range climbed by 30 per cent, owing to the high temperatures' has less appeal than 'Another 30,000 hot, thirsty people were drinking Fizzipop'.

# FINAL CHECKLIST FOR BOTH OE AND SE SPEAKERS

If you try to improve in all 10 areas at the same time, you will probably forget your own name.

So decide which *one* of the 10 ideas could improve your performance in your next international meeting, re-read that section, and commit yourself to it.

*'X' for commitment*

1. Grade your language
   (I will take my partner's linguistic abilities into account)                    _____

2. Use the full range of tone and tempo
   (I will put a little music and colour into my speech)                    _____

3. Accentuate the positive
   (I will be careful with irony and understatement)                    _____

4. Show warmth; show willingness
   (I will be the first to break the ice, by word and gesture)                    _____

5. Use questions to good effect
   (I will remember the persuasive power of questions, and use it)                    _____

6. Keep it short and simple – sometimes
   (I will make my sentences short. I will put one idea in each)                    _____

7. Use big, bold signposts
   (I will make sure my listener knows exactly where we are in the argument)                    _____

8. Summarize often
   (I will pause and take stock regularly, for everybody's sake)                    _____

9. Don't worry about body language
   (I will behave naturally and be myself)                    _____

10. Add a little spice
    (I will find opportunities to bring my message to life)                    _____

# APPENDIX 6A – OUR OFFSHORE VERSION OF THE LANGUAGE QUIZ

1. As you know, our competitors have had an advantage recently.
2. I think it'll be very difficult to remove him. Do you have a gun?
3. I know that you're more experienced than me in this field, but could I suggest that you look at the options again?
4. Can I say something before you begin?
5. At last! Where were you?

# A Glossary of Offshore English

The final section of this book is dedicated to more detailed observations on Offshore English. We begin with an example of how communication can suffer when everyday words shift their meaning.

## 'CROSS PURPOSES' – A DRAMA IN ONE ACT

*Somewhere in Europe, Bob, a native speaker of English, is nearing the end of a meeting with Rene, a Continental European:*

| | | |
|---|---|---|
| 1 | *Bob:* | How long are you here for, Rene? |
| 2 | *Rene:* | Since last night. |
| 3 | *Bob:* | No, I mean when do you have to leave for the airport? |
| 4 | *Rene:* | Oh. 12 o'clock at the latest. |
| 5 | *Bob:* | Well in that case, we'd better press on. |
| 6 | *Rene:* | Sorry? |
| 7 | *Bob:* | Let's resume, shall we, or would you like some more coffee? |
| 8 | *Rene:* | No, let's resume. Would you like to? |
| 9 | *Bob:* | What? |
| 10 | *Rene:* | Resume. |
| 11 | *Bob:* | Yes, suits me. (A long silence, as Bob fiddles with his papers, and Rene gazes out of the window. Bob looks up.) Over to you, then. |
| 12 | *Rene:* | Ah! Yes! Well perhaps we could turn to the new quality control system. You say it's slowing things down . . . |
| 13 | *Bob:* | That's right. This week, for example, we're already two days late for one of my regular customers – half a dozen XB90s . . . |
| 14 | *Rene:* | Not an important order, then? |
| 15 | *Bob:* | I think it is! |
| 16 | *Rene:* | If you say so . . . What's your usual delivery delay on XB90s? |
| 17 | *Bob:* | No delay at all, if I can help it. |
| 18 | *Rene:* | But how much time do you need to turn an order round? |
| 19 | *Bob:* | We quote 14 days. It's all there in the report . . . |

| 20 | *Rene:* | And how long does it actually take? |
| 21 | *Bob:* | Fourteen days, of course! What sort of operation do you think I'm running? Look, I'm sure we can all see benefits coming from a really effective control system, but . . . |
| 22 | *Rene:* | I think it's a bit early to talk about benefits, don't you? |
| 23 | *Bob:* | (Now quite exasperated) It was you who persuaded me 12 months ago to invest in the damn thing. Now you're casting doubt on the whole exercise. Terrific! Really terrific! |
| 24 | *Rene:* | I think that's an exaggeration, Bob. There's no real cause for alarm . . . |

Can you feel Bob and Rene's frustration? If you want to work out what's going wrong, turn to the glossary on pages 138–47 and look up the words *since, resume, important, delay, actually, benefits* and *terrific* – the stumbling blocks which first appear in lines 2, 7, 14, 16, 20, 21 and 23 respectively of the dialogue above.

Standard English (SE) is a hybrid language; it has drawn on Continental originals at various times in its history. Down the centuries, certain Standard words have developed strains different from their Continental cousins. Many of the terms treated in this glossary are close to their pre-English roots.

A German recognizes the word 'meaning' as closely related to *Meinung* (opinion), and is naturally inclined to use it in similar ways; likewise the Italian who uses 'sympathetic' as he uses its Italian cousin *simpalico* (nice). These hidden traps in the English language are so abundant that the French have a special term for them: *les faux amis* (false friends) – words that seem to mean the same but do not.

Japanese or Hungarian readers might be perplexed by some of the examples in this glossary, since their native languages are remote from SE, and offer few opportunities for *interference* to take place. ('Interference' describes the involuntary transferring of a word or construction from one language to another.) However, they might find the glossary useful when they are perplexed by what a Colombian or an Austrian says to them in his version of English.

Many innovations in Offshore English (OE) have occurred where interference from other languages is so frequent that it has produced an acceptable form – the 'common practice' line so common in linguistic development.

This effect is likely in cases where the deviation from Standard carries no penalty. For example, 'Telephone to me' is prescriptively 'wrong', and teachers of English work hard to eradicate the 'error' in their foreign students. Yet if the students are studying English in a practical rather than an academic spirit, they find it hard to care. The construction is clear and unambiguous, and causes no pain to other Offshore speakers, so why worry? (Similarly 'I will pay my groceries'; 'Can we meet us at 2.30?'; 'How much did you buy that?' and many others.)

Often the OE meaning of an individual word corresponds to a subsidiary meaning in SE, or to a usage that now seems antiquated. (So the OE 'pretend' is close to the SE 'The Young Pretender's claim to the throne' while the rather Dickensian 'I remarked that he stank of garlic, but decided to say nothing' uses the verb exactly like the OE 'remark'.)

Offshore often shrugs off distinctions in Standard which are hard to fathom and bring little benefit in terms of communication. Many Continental languages make no distinction between 'make' and 'do', 'let' and 'leave' or 'like' and 'as' – one word does the job perfectly well. The Offshore practitioner tends to use the words interchangeably.

Sometimes it is not the *meaning* of the word which is at issue, but its *connotations* (eg, the wartime associations of 'collaborator'), or its force (eg, 'satisfactory', which carries far more positive feeling in OE than in SE).

This glossary is aimed principally at native SE speakers. It throws light on some of the confusions which lurk beneath the surface of Offshore conversations, especially with Continental partners. It will also be useful to non-native speakers who want to be sure that their messages are both 'correct' and clear.

## THE GLOSSARY ITSELF

The glossary concentrates on individual words, with occasional cross-references to other parts of this chapter (eg, 'Time').

The definition or explanation given first in each case relates to Offshore. The material in square brackets clarifies Standard usage, but does not offer a full definition of the word: that is the job of a proper dictionary or an English teacher.

Where appropriate, we have indicated 'language of origin' with the international symbols (D for Germany, E for Spain, etc). If there is no such indication, the usage is widespread.

We have subjective opinions about the items in this glossary. Some of them seem ugly, but are likely to survive and even supplant Standard terms (eg, 'rentability'). Others are quite inoffensive to the English ear, yet they will probably remain 'incorrect' (eg, 'formation').

Just as the world's business lingua franca has absorbed much of its vocabulary from American corporate English in the last few generations, so the resurgence of a united Europe could reverse the traffic a little: international meetings in Chicago might begin to accept a pan-European view on the real meaning of 'eventually'.

**D** = Germany **E** = Spain **F** = France **I** = Italy **S** = Sweden

**Abbreviations** are often pronounced as words – so *f.o.b.* (free on board) is *fob*. Similarly *cif, vip, ira* and even *rip*. [All these are pronounced letter-by-letter in SE.]

**Achieve,** *finish*, as in 'We have achieved the project.' [*Reach*, as in 'We have achieved our objective.']

**Actions,** *shares*, as in 'I sold my actions at just the right moment'.

**Actual,** *current*, as in 'our actual Personnel Director', [*Real*, as in 'Our actual sales in 1989 were better than we expected'.]

**Actually,** *at the moment*, as in 'They are reviewing the situation actually.' [*In fact*, as in 'Actually, my name is Jane not Jean.']

**Advices,** *see* **Informations**

**Agenda,** *diary*, as in 'Let me look in my agenda.' **D** [The *order of business*, as in 'How can we cover this agenda in two hours?']

**Aggress,** *attack*, as in: 'He aggressed me so I walked out of the meeting.' **F** [OE invention; there is no such verb in SE. 'He was aggressive' exists.]

**Agree,** often 'I am agree', or 'I am agreed' in OE. A good example of a deep-rooted 'error' which in no way disturbs communication.

**All right,** *see* **Satisfactory**

**Anonymous,** sometimes used to describe a company with anonymous shareholders, ie, a public company. (From *société anonyme*, etc.)

**Apparently,** 1. *obviously*, as in 'Would you like to improve productivity?' – 'Apparently!' **F**
2. *Only apparently*, as in 'Apparently he accepted my advice, but I don't think he was listening'. **I** [*It seems*, or *People are saying*, as in 'Apparently our competitors are in financial trouble'.]

**As,** *see* **Like**.

**Assist,** *attend*, as in 'Can you assist to the conference?' **F** [*Help*, as in 'He assisted me at a difficult moment'.]

**At last,** *lastly*, with no dramatic overtones, as in 'And at last it is time to fix a date for the next meeting.' **D** [In SE, there is a sense of tension and relief, as in 'At last you are here! We had almost lost hope.']

**Benefit,** *profit*, as in 'a record benefit' **F** [*Advantage*, as in 'The benefits can't be measured in financial terms'.]

**By**, *see* 'Time' (p121)

**Cannot**, *see* 'Contractions' (p121)

**Charge**, *load*, as in 'I didn't know the gun [or the ship] was charged.' [*Demand* a price, as in 'This supplier is charging us too much'.]

**Chapter**, *heading*, as in 'I think we should print all the chapters in block capitals' **I** [SE has drifted further from the Latin *caput*, and now uses 'chapter' to mean 'section' of a book. So 'chapter headings' is reasonable.]

**Collaborator**, *colleague*, as in 'I must give credit to all collaborators'. [Connotation: *traitor*, as in 'The collaborators were punished when the occupying army had retreated'.]

**Comfortable**, *convenient*, as in 'A 10.30 appointment is quite comfortable for me'.

**Compensate**, *compensate for*, as in 'Big sales at Christmas compensated the bad summer'. *See* 'Prepositions' (p121)

**Competence**, 1. *competition*, as in 'We are facing serious competence'. **E** 2. *Span of control*, as in the traditional, but often forgotten SE usage 'This project is outside my competence.' **D, I**

**Competent**, *able*, or *well qualified*, as in 'They tell me the anaesthetist is competent' **S** [This statement in SE is not what you want to hear as they wheel you to the operating theatre. It means he is not completely useless, but not very good at his job.]

**Concurrent**, *competitor*, as in 'We must watch our concurrents carefully', [*Simultaneous*, as in 'The advertising campaign will run concurrently with the special price promotion'.]

**Conductor**, *driver*. [Ticket collector or inspector, on public transport in most English-speaking cities.]

**Conference**, *lesson*, or *presentation*, as in 'He made an excellent conference and nobody fell asleep'.

**Control**, *check*, as in 'From time to time I control his expenses claims.' [*Direct*, as in 'I am not too old to control the department!'] So 'quality control' in SE gives a mental picture of continuous management of all factors affecting quality, while in OE it suggests a sampling procedure at some late stage of the production process.

**Curiosity**, *curious item or fact*, as in 'I found several curiosities in the annual report'. [In SE, this usage is obsolete. Dickens wrote *The Old Curiosity Shop* a long time ago.]

**Damn**, the strongest swear-word recommended in OE. 'Bloody' always sounds strange in a non-SE accent, and is anyway difficult to define. Anything stronger, in religious, lavatorial or sexual terms, is avoided by the OE user who wants to be on the safe side.

**Daughter company**, *subsidiary*, **D** With its companion 'Mother company', it has a friendly feel which might displace the rather bald SE terms. *See* **Holding**.

**Definite**, *final*, as in 'She has definitely closed down the factory.' [*Certain*, as in 'We have no definite candidates yet'.]

**Delay**, *lead time*, as in 'How long is your usual delay on this product?' **F** [Lateness, as in 'We apologize for the delay, which is partly due to a fire in our factory'.]

**Demand**, *ask for*, as in 'I offered them coffee or tea, and most of them demanded tea'. **F** [Stronger in SE, as in 'The terrorists demanded the release of their comrades'.]

**Design**, *draw*, as in 'He designed his company organization chart on the back of a menu'. **F** [*Create/engineer*, as in 'He designs uniforms for airline staff/'Who designed this damn equipment?']

**Dismiss**, *resign*, as in 'She had an argument with her boss and dismissed the company'. **F** [*Fire/sack*, as in 'He dismissed me when I failed to reach my targets'.]

**Do**, *see* **Make**

**During**, *see* 'Time' (p121)

**Economy**, *finance*, as in 'Lars Olsson, Chief Executive, Economy' **S** [Used in SE either of 'the Brazilian economy', or as in 'We must cut costs; can you suggest any economies?']

**Employee**, often suggests a higher position in the company than the SE equivalent. This is more a matter of connotation than of definition. Experienced OE users know very well that ranks and grades and levels of power are difficult to express in one word, just as it is impossible to translate quickly and accurately from one legal system (or educational system) to another.

**Engaged**, *committed* as in 'We appreciate the engagement of your staff, who made us feel very welcome' **F** [*Hired* as in 'We engaged a new firm of auditors'.]

**Enjoy**, *often* 'I am enjoyed'. (*see* **Agree**)

**Equipments**, *see* **Informations**

**Eventually**, *perhaps*, as in 'We expect a return of 15, eventually 16, per cent'. *After a considerable time* as in 'Be patient; eventually this investment will give a good return'.]

**Excuse**, *apology*, as in 'I'm too busy to come to the meeting; please make excuses for me'. **F** [*Justification* (often empty), as in 'I don't accept your stupid excuses. You threw the ball; the ball broke the window'.]

**Exercise**, *financial year*, as in 'We expect a recession to start during this exercise' **F** [*Experimental project* or *manoeuvre*, as in 'The whole exercise was a waste of time and money'.]

**Expect**, *wait*, as in 'I'll go and find somebody to help. You expect me here'. **I**

**Experience**, *see* **Experiment**

**Experiment**, with **Experience**, one of a classic pair of false friends. **F** So OE can produce: 'Some of our most experimented researchers conducted the experience'. [SE has the two ideas in reverse.]

**Figures,** *diagrams*, as in 'The figures in this report tell us very little about the numbers involved'. [*Numbers*, as in 'I have a poor head for figures'.]

**For**, sometimes *because*, as in 'I cut the meeting short for I was in a hurry'. **D** [This is rather an old-fashioned use of 'for' in SE.]

**For**, *by*, as in 'our profits are up for 5 per cent'. *See* 'Prepositions' (p121)

**Formation**, *training*, as in 'We have cut the budget for formation'. **F** [*Layout*, as in 'an interesting geological formation'.]

**Funny**, *enjoyable*, as in 'The party at your house was rather funny'. [*Amusing*, as in 'He made a very funny after-dinner speech', or *strange*, as in 'He has a funny attitude to women'.] (Even Abba, the Swedish pop group, used OE for this one:
'Money, money, money
Must be funny
In a rich man's world'.)

**Furnisher**, *supplier*, as in 'You are not the only furnisher of such services, you know . . .' **F** [*Supplier of furniture*, as in 'Have you seen the office furnishers' catalogue anywhere? I need a new filing cabinet'.]

**Furnitures**, *see* **Informations**

**Get**, a nightmare word in OE. Since it means everything and nothing in SE, and there is always a more precise alternative, OE prefers 'acquiring information' to 'getting information', and in OE we 'become old' while in SE we 'get old'.

**Great**, *big*, as in 'I don't like them, but they are a great company'. **D** [*Excellent*, as in I'm staying in a great little hotel'.]

**Hardly**, often *hard* or *forcefully*, as in 'He presented his argument hardly'. [In SE, the idiomatic construction 'I have hardly any money' means 'I have almost no money'. The adverb from 'hard' is 'hard'.]

**History**, often *story*, as in 'Have you heard the history about the travelling salesman . . .?' **F, I** [*Record of the past*, as in 'The History of Ancient Rome'.]

**Holding**, *holding company*, as in 'Our holding is in Liechtenstein, but our operational headquarters is in Amsterdam'. OE, largely under French influence, sometimes abbreviates. So a 'self-service restaurant' in Paris has become 'un sell'. *See* 'Parts of Speech' (p121)

**How long**, *see* 'Time' (p121)

**Important**, often simply *large*, as in 'This is not an important investment, but it means life or death for the company'. **F** [*Significant*, as in 'Small details are very important in this job'.]

**In case**, often *if*, as in 'In case it rains, we will cancel the garden party'. **F** [*As a precaution*, as in 'We have hired a tent for the garden party in case it rains'.]

**Incoherent**, often *inconsistent*, as in 'You have made three incoherent statements'. **F** [*Over-emotional and illogical*, as in 'He was so angry his speech became incoherent'.]

**Informations,** OE plural of 'information', as in 'He gave me three useful information'. Most languages have plurals also for 'advice', 'equipment', 'furniture', 'news', and so OE often uses them too. [For a plural, SE has 'pieces of advice/equipment/etc'.]

**Interesting**, *financially worthwhile*, as in 'It's a standard project, but very interesting'. **F** [*Fascinating*, as in 'She lent me an interesting book'.]

**Investigate**, often *invest*, as in 'Have we investigated the money wisely?' **D** [Sherlock Holmes *investigates* crimes.]

**Invite**, often *stand treat*, as in 'You paid for lunch yesterday. I invite you this time'. **F** [SE has idioms like 'This is on me', or 'Let me stand you lunch'. 'Invite' is mainly reserved for 'They invited me home for the weekend' etc.]

**Issue**, *outcome*, as in 'What was the issue of the meeting? I had to leave before the end. [*Discussion point*, as in 'I'd rather not mention that issue in public'.]

**Leave**, *see* **Let**

**Lecture**, *reading*, as in 'He didn't understand the class when the professor was speaking, but he found the lecture easier'. [*Lesson*, as in 'I have to miss the nine o'clock lecture'.]

**Let**, largely interchangeable with 'leave', since most languages have one word here for both SE meanings. So OE can produce 'He let the lights switched on all night'. [In SE, 'leave' is close to 'forget'/ 'ignore', as in 'Don't leave the decision to me!'; 'let' is more like 'permit', as in 'Shall we let the secret out?']

**Like**, largely interchangeable with 'as', since most languages make do with one word for both sets of SE meanings. So OE can produce 'Really intelligent people, as my boss . . .' [In SE, this example requires 'doing', as a near-synonym for 'performing'.]

**Make**, largely interchangeable with 'do', since most languages use one word to cover what SE sees as two distinct concepts. So OE can produce 'They are making their homework'. [In SE, this example requires 'doing', as a near-synonym for 'performing'.]

**Many**, *see* **Much**

**Matter**, used often in OE, as in 'What do you think about that matter?' [Where SE would be satisfied with 'What do you think about that?']

**Mean**, *believe*. *See* **Meaning**

**Meaning**, *opinion*, as in 'We have different meanings'. **D** Even in OE, this usage will probably not take hold.

**Mother company**, *parent company*. *See* **Daughter company, D**

**Much**, with 'many', used in preference to 'a lot of', as in 'He made much money and many enemies'. [In conversational SE, 'much' and 'many' are common in the interrogative and the negative, as in 'How much?' and 'Not many'. In the affirmative, 'a lot of wine'/'a lot of bottles' is more frequent.]

**Must**, *see* 'Obligation' (p122)

**Nearly**, *approximately*, as in 'One hundred Hungarian forints is worth nearly one pound sterling'. [In SE, *almost*, as in 'The shock nearly killed me'.]

**Necessary**, used in preference to tricky modals like 'need' or 'should'. 'Is it necessary to leave a tip?' might sound ponderous to native SE speakers, but it serves the purpose in OE, and is regular and easy to handle.

**Newses**, *see* **Informations**

**OK**, *excellent*, as in 'Thank you very much. Your hospitality was OK'. [Similar to 'satisfactory' and 'all right', which in SE usually mean 'tolerable'.]

**Other,** often *different*, as in 'His feelings are other'. **D** [In SE, 'The other thing' might be exactly the same as 'this thing' – separate, but not different.]

**Obviously**, *see* **Apparently**

**Of course!**, *certainly!*, as in 'Are you ready for lunch?' – 'Of course!' [*Naturally! Why do you ask?*, as in 'Do you really believe in your product?' – 'Of course!']

**One**, often used, especially by Spanish speakers, as the unemphatic indefinite article in place of SE 'a/an' – as in 'they made one offer for the goods'. [SE usually reserves 'one' for emphasizing unity or singularity, as in 'Give me one good reason to accept your offer']

**Particular**, often *strange*, as in 'Waiter, this fish tastes rather particular'. **F** [Overlap with SE 'peculiar'.]

**Partner**, an increasingly popular term in OE, especially among Germans, to refer to anyone you have dealings with, suggestive of harmony and understanding. So 'My supplier/client/banker/opposite number/agent' is becoming 'my partner'. SE has no good equivalent to this use of 'partner', so we have adopted it in this book.

**Peculiar**, *see* **Particular**

**Piece**, *unit*, as in 'The market for Easter eggs is enormous. We expect to sell half a million pieces this year'.

**Politics**, often *policy*, as in 'We have very strict politics on this matter'. [In SE, 'politics' is either an academic subject or a dirty game.]

**Possible**, used in preference to tricky modals like 'can' or 'might': 'Is it possible to use your phone?' might sound ponderous to SE native speakers, but it works fine in OE.

**Possibly**, *if possible*, as in 'I'll fax you the information tomorrow, possibly'. **I** [In SE this sounds casual and uncaring – 'maybe I will, maybe I won't'.]

**Preservative**, *condom*. The French are greatly amused by English marmalade labels: 'This product contains preservatives'.

**Pretend**, *aspire*, as in 'We are pretending to market the best-quality product'. [*Simulate*, as in 'He pretended to be asleep, but he was listening to every word'.]

**Prevision,** *forecast*, as in 'The market previsions for Hungary are optimistic'. **F, I** [The word does not yet exist in SE.]

**Problem,** often *item* or *issue*, with no gloomy connotations, as in 'We have discussed this problem enough; we must move on to the areas of difficulty'. [In SE, 'problem' always has unpleasant connotations, as in 'Problems, problems, problems! Can't you think positive for a moment?']

**Profit,** *see* **Benefit**

**Protocol,** often *minutes,* as in 'I hope you all received the protocol of the last meeting'. **D** [Correct procedure, as in 'Does anybody know the protocol for dinner with an Irish Archbishop and a Saudi prince?']

**Quite,** sometimes *absolutely* where it sounds like 'fairly', as in 'The results were quite good. Open the champagne . . .' [In SE, 'quite' means 'totally' with absolute adjectives – 'quite perfect' or 'quite incredible'. It only means 'fairly' or 'rather' with scalar adjectives – 'quite heavy' or 'quite well-written'.]

**Realize,** *make real*, as in 'They realized a big civil engineering project'. [*Understand*, as in 'I suddenly realized the scope of the problem'.]

**Red numbers,** *the red*, as in 'I'm afraid we're writing red numbers again'. **D** [SE is more economical – 'We're in the red'.]

**Remark,** often *notice*, as in 'I remarked that nobody else was formally dressed, but said nothing'. [*Passed comment*, as in 'She remarked to him that his prices were rather high'.]

**Resume**, usually *sum up*, as in 'The chairman resumed very succinctly'. **F** [Recommence, as in 'We'll resume after coffee'.]

**Rentability,** *profitability*, as in 'a high-volume product with low rentability'. **F** [The word does not yet exist in SE.]

**Responsible,** *the responsible person*, as in 'Could I speak to the responsible of management training, please?' Many adjectives in many Continental languages can be used without an accompanying noun – eg Hugo's *Les Miserables*, which translates rather uncomfortably into SE as 'The Miserable Ones'.

**Safe,** often *secure*, as in 'He wanted a safe job, so he became a policeman in New York'. [In SE, 'safety' is usually a physical matter.]

**Satisfactory,** often carries stronger praise than in SE, as in 'Your contribution to the meeting was satisfactory'. In OE, such a statement is cause for congratulations. The same goes for 'Your samples seem to be all right'. [In SE, 'satisfactory' and 'all right' are used to describe things in a less positive way, as in 'The food was all right, but I could have cooked it better myself'.]

**Say,** *see* **Tell**

**Sensible,** often *sensitive*, as in 'The market is very sensible to interest rates on loans'. [*Reasonable/well-balanced*, as in 'No fantasies, please: I want sensible suggestions'.]

**Shortly,** often *briefly*, as in 'please tell us the basic facts shortly'. **D** [*Soon*, as in 'Lunch will be served shortly'.]

**Since,** often *for*, as in 'I have known him since several years'. *See* 'Time' (p121)

**Society,** often *company*, as in 'before I joined my present society' **F, I** [Organization with voluntary members, eg Royal Society for Protection of Birds.]

**Spare,** *save*, as in 'We can spare a little money by making it in plastic'. **D** [Give something from reserves, eg 'Can you spare some money for this charity?']

**Summary,** sometimes *contents list*. **F**

**Speak,** *see* **Tell**

**Sympathetic,** *pleasant*, or *easy to get on with*, as in 'He never offers to pay for lunch; I don't find him sympathetic'. [*Kind to people in trouble*, as in 'Thank you for listening so sympathetically to my problems'.]

**Talk,** *see* **Tell**

**Technique,** often *technology*, as in 'Bengt specializes in data transmission technique'. **S** [*Skill* or *method*, as in 'She always beats me at tennis; she has a very good backhand technique'.]

**Tell,** with 'say', 'speak' and 'talk', forms a group whose shades of meaning are often lost in OE. So SE 'Tell me . . .' can easily become 'Say me . . .' and so on. **I**

**Terrific,** often *frightening*, as in 'I don't like terrific movies'. **F** [Usually *very good*, as in 'This sushi fish is terrific'.]

**Therefore,** *that's why*, as in 'We need a specialist for this job. Therefore I sent for you'. **D** [In SE, 'therefore' is used to introduce an idea which is new to the listener, as in 'The offer is a fair one. We therefore recommend that you accept it'.]

**Until,** sometimes *by*, as in 'I promise to let you have the figures until lunchtime tomorrow'. **D**. *See* 'Time' (p121)

**Used to,** a minefield. To give just one example: OE 'I use to spend my weekends gardening' probably means SE 'I usually spend . . .'

**Vivacious,** *hard wearing*, as in 'Our tractor tyres are very vivacious'. **F** [*Full of life* or – in Hollywood – *sexy*, as in 'a vivacious blonde starlet'.]

**When,** often *if*, as in 'When you agree with me . . .' **D** [The SE distinction here is also an important one in many other languages, and will probably survive in 'correct' OE.]

**With pleasure!,** *Yes, please!* **F**

**Word, give the,** *hand over to*, as in 'That's all from me. I'll give the word to Dr Mueller'.

**Wrong, you are,** *I'm afraid I can't agree. See* 'Register' (p122)

**Yes,** covers a range of meanings from 'You are absolutely right and I agree to do as you suggest' to 'I am listening to what you are saying but reserving judgment until I work out what you really mean'. For cultural rather than linguistic reasons, this latter meaning is especially common among the Japanese. We can only suggest you check from time to time.

# Final Quiz

These are all true stories. We have omitted commercially sensitive detail. The answers to the questions follow immediately on pages 151–3.

## 1. What is a contract?

How would you define the word *contract?*

At a Canning seminar for one of the world's largest computer services companies, managers from the USA, France, Italy, the UK and the Netherlands were asked the same question. Match the answer to the country:

a.   an insurance document for use if things get really bad;

b.   a prison;

c.   a list of protocols which can be interpreted in many different ways;

d.   a Bible.

## 2. Can I trust you?

The head of corporate law at one of Turkey's biggest conglomerates had spent a year negotiating a joint venture contract with an Egyptian manufacturer to produce steel wire for radial tyres. The contract had specified that the Egyptians would build a £50 million factory and that the Turks would take 100 per cent of the output. Contract documentation was highly detailed and comprehensive.

Six months after the contract was signed everything seemed to be going well. The lawyer got a visit from the head of the Egyptian company. The Egyptian threw the thick contract onto the Turk's desk and said: '*These terms are impossible. I can't live with them*'. It became clear that he had only just read the contract in full.

What would you have done if you had been the Turkish lawyer?

## 3. My company is the best!

An Englishman, general manager of his company's Italian subsidiary for the past 14 years, was at a meeting in Milan. It was the inaugural session of a network of professional service companies who wanted to pool their skills in order to offer their clients a wider range of services. Each delegate had been asked to prepare a brief presentation of his or her company.

The Englishman was annoyed to find the other delegates ignoring the request for brevity; many over-ran by 20 minutes. When it was his turn to speak, he delivered a two-minute speech (in fluent Italian). It had a clear message, was well structured, and gave the key information relevant to his listeners. However there was an awkward silence when he sat down, and then a minimum of polite applause. The meeting finished two hours late and the Englishman left it feeling it had all been a complete waste of time.

On reflection, and after chatting to an Italian friend who had been present at the meeting, the Englishman realized that he should have taken a different approach. What should he have done and why?

### 4. It's a deal . . . isn't it?

Two firms in the brewing industry, one Dutch and the other Japanese, were in the final stage of negotiating a joint venture contract. There were certain minor details on which neither side was prepared to concede. It was late Sunday afternoon in one of the Japanese company's breweries, and a break for refreshments was called. The Dutch asked for cold beers. The Japanese left the room and instead of the usual ten-minute time-out, they stayed away for an hour. When they came back, the leader of the Japanese team bowed deeply and said they were now prepared to accept all the remaining demands from the Dutch side. The Dutch were amazed but delighted. The two sides shook hands and that evening the exhausted negotiators celebrated with the help of the company's products.

The Dutch congratulated themselves on their negotiating skills. Should they have been so pleased? Why had the Japanese changed tack so suddenly? How committed was the Japanese company to the contract and the relationship?

### 5. Let's meet!

It was an important internal meeting at the Finnish head office, and it should have started 10 minutes ago. The two Finns – one woman and one man – and the German had all arrived over 15 minutes ago. They were waiting for a Chinese woman from the Beijing office and a Frenchman who just starting a two-year assignment in Finland. The German had twice broken the silence in the room with a proposal that they should start their business discussion. The Finns had grunted and nodded, but seemed prepared to wait. The Chinese woman and the Frenchman finally arrived together. She said little except to apologize for being late;

the Frenchman also apologized but immediately began some story about going to the wrong building in Espoo.

The Finnish woman interrupted the Frenchman's discourse and briskly suggested that they agree on the agenda for the meeting. The German and the Frenchman took out their pocket diaries, and seemed perplexed when she started to outline the day's business. The German then produced a print-out of the e-mail he had sent to everybody three days before: his proposed list of discussion points. Both Finns had a copy of the e-mail; some points had been crossed out and others added. The German asked them why they had not let him know in advance about the alterations, so he could prepare himself properly. The Finnish woman apologized but did not explain. The Frenchman denied having received the e-mail. Nobody asked the Chinese woman whether she had received the e-mail; she was left fiddling with some papers from her briefcase. The other Finn sat tapping away on his laptop having said nothing more than '*hello*' so far . . .

How well is the meeting going? What cultural differences does this description reveal?

## FINAL QUIZ: ANSWERS

### 1. What is a contract?

One of the Americans said: '*A contract is my Bible. I always carry the relevant one in my briefcase. So do all my staff.*' The Italian looked straight at the American: '*A contract is a prison*'! he said with considerable passion, forming a cage with his hands. One of the Frenchmen shrugged and talked about the need for '*protocols which could be interpreted in many different ways*'. The Dutch, after conferring among themselves, stated that a contract was '*an insurance document which should only be referred to if things got really bad.*' The British agreed with the Dutch.

### 2. Can I trust you?

The Turkish lawyer studied the Egyptian's face and tried to assess how much he could trust him. He then picked up the contract, tore it up and threw it in the waste basket. The Egyptian thanked him and they moved on to talk about non-business matters. Two years later the Turk was able to report to us that the joint venture was still very successful.

The Egyptian comes from a culture which still views an oral promise as more binding than any written contract (agreeing with the Italian in 1: a contract is a prison). He would prefer to work in a way that allows both sides to renegotiate terms as the project moves forward and circumstances change. A similar attitude prevails across much of Asia and Africa:

successful business relationships are built upon personal relationships where there is mutual trust. This does not mean that negotiations are any less tough than they would be in, say, the USA or Northern Europe.

### 3. My company is the best!

The Englishman had momentarily forgotten all that he had learnt about Italy. For example, the education system in Italy encourages Italians to be eloquent and positive, and to speak for however long is necessary to demonstrate that they have thought of all the points – directly or obliquely relevant. Italian school examinations are partly oral. In the UK, by contrast, examinations are almost entirely written, and often involve summarizing complicated texts.

Most British people are intolerant of boasters. The English expert on nuclear physics will say that he knows '*a few things*' about the subject; a fellow Brit will interpret this correctly. The Italian or American will take him at his word, and then get upset when they hear that he won the Nobel prize last year.

The Englishman should have spoken for longer about his company's expertise and results, sprinkling his presentation with the names of prestigious clients and stories of corporate success.

### 4. It's a deal . . . isn't it?

In Japan you only drink alcohol when the deal is agreed. The Japanese delegation interpreted the Dutch request for alcohol as: *accept our demands or the deal is off*. However the Dutch triumph was short-lived: the Japanese negotiators had agreed to the deal without first consulting anyone at head office, simply because nobody was there on Sunday afternoon. Several departments in the Japanese company later refused to abide by the concessions which the negotiators had made and the relationship with the Dutch was soon soured.

### 5. Let's meet!

Things could have been a lot worse.

It is very difficult for a Finn or a German to respect someone who cannot control his own time, or does not take punctuality seriously. Canning's own research shows that the French consider themselves to be even less punctual than the Italians. The Frenchman's apology is not deeply meant; rather he is offended by the Finnish woman's interruption as he is warming to his story: this insistence on getting down to business is narrow-minded, he feels.

Both the Frenchman and the German have a problem with the word *agenda:* see *Glossary*, page 138).

The Finn with the laptop is not being rude, by Finnish standards. He has nothing important to say, so while the others work out the agenda, he is using the time constructively.

The German wants to stick to the agenda for which he has prepared himself. The Finns want to get things clear at the start of the meeting. The Frenchman knows that whatever the official agenda for a meeting, there is always a more important hidden agenda.

And the Chinese woman? She is wondering when she is going to be asked to introduce herself and read out the statement she has scripted in advance. Meanwhile she is having great difficulty understanding the strange accents in which her European colleagues speak English.

# Further Reading

Axtell, Roger E (1985) *Do's & Taboos Around the World*, Parker Pen

Bartlett, Christopher A and Ghoshal (1989), *Sumatra Managing Across Borders*, Harvard

Barzini, Luigi (1983) *The Europeans*, Penguin

Brake, Terence (1997) *The Global Leader*, Irwin

Carlisle, John and Parker, Robert (1989) *Beyond Negotiation*, John Wiley

Hall, Edward T (1959) *The Silent Language*, Doubleday; (1976) *Beyond Culture*, Doubleday

Hendon, Donald W (1989) *How to Negotiate Worldwide*, Gower

Hickson, David J and Pugh, Dereck S (1995) *Management Worldwide*, Penguin

Hill, Richard (1994) *Euromanagers & Martians*, Europublications

Hoecklin, Lisa (1994) *Managing Cultural Differences*, Addison-Wesley/E.I.U.

Hofstede, Geert (1980) *Culture's Consequences*, (1991) Sage; *Cultures & Organisations*, McGraw-Hill

Hutton, John (1998) *The World of the International Manager*, Philip Allen

Lewis, Richard D (1996) *When Cultures Collide*, Brealey

Mole, John (1997) *Mind Your Manners*, Brealey

Porter, Michael (1990) *The Competitive Advantage of Nations*, Macmillan

Seelye, H Ned and Seelye-James, Alan (1995) *Culture Clash*, NTC

Trompenaars, Fons (1994) *Riding the Waves of Culture*, Brealy

# Index